D1596908

IMAGES
of America

WASHINGTON
NORTH CAROLINA

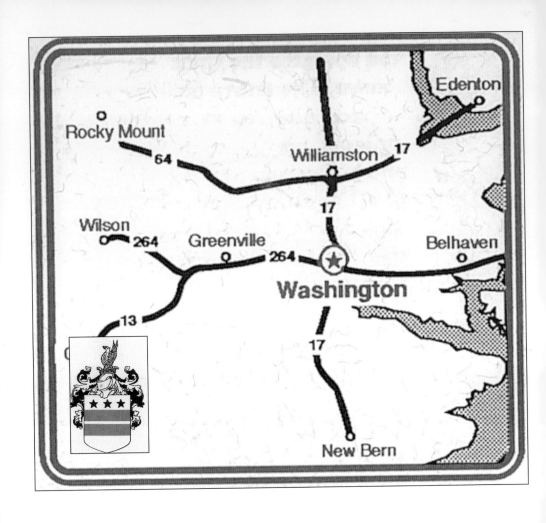

Cover: The Washington High School Marching Band is leading a fall parade down Market Street to Main Street in 1948. See page 43 for more information.

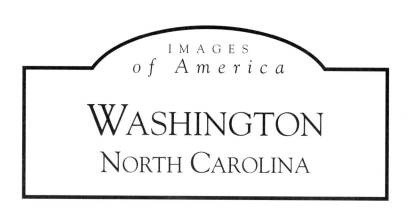

IMAGES
of America

WASHINGTON
NORTH CAROLINA

Louis Van Camp

ARCADIA

Published by Arcadia Publishing,
an imprint of Tempus Publishing, Inc.
2 Cumberland Street
Charleston, SC 29401

Printed in Great Britain.

Library of Congress Catalog Card Number: 99-069533

For all general information contact Arcadia Publishing at:
Telephone 843-853-2070
Fax 843-853-0044
E-Mail sales@arcadiapublishing.com

For customer service and orders:
Toll-Free 1-888-313-2665

Visit us on the internet at http://www.arcadiapublishing.com

Dedication

*This book is dedicated to all the wonderful people of Washington
who strive to preserve their past history, yet build for the future.*

Images of America: Washington North Carolina *is a pictorial documenation. Much of the
information was supplied by several founding families and is therefore believed to be reliable.*

CONTENTS

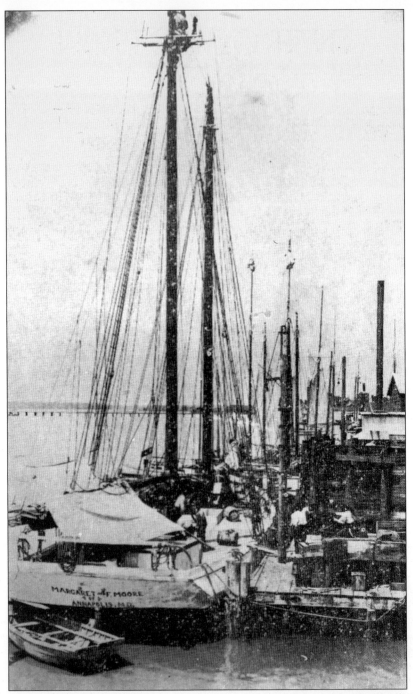

The Chesapeake Bay schooner *Margaret F. Moore* from Annapolis, Maryland, is loading barrels of potatoes at a Washington pier, probably at the Fowle dock at the foot of Respess Street, in 1906. The 6- to 8-foot draft of these vessels made them ideal for the Pamlico River because the river shoaled on every storm, making it difficult to maintain a constant channel depth. Havens Oil Co. (cotton seed oil) is the building with the smoke stack in the background. (PC OS.)

INTRODUCTION

Washington 1790. Washington is located at the junction of the Tar River, where it broadens and becomes the Pamlico River. By 1790, this advantageous location was recognized by Northern industrialists who wanted to export their products to the inland cities of Greenville, Tarboro, Wilson, Rocky Mount, and Raleigh. In return, Beaufort County merchants and farmers would export their vast virgin lumber supply and agricultural products to the North. During the Revolutionary War, Washington became a naval supply depot for Washington's Army. The port of Washington became an official Custom Clearing House for shipping by 1796. That year, the Custom House reported 130 vessels had entered the Port of Washington (then a city of about 536 people). Lumber eventually became the primary export industry of Eastern North Carolina because of the millions of acres of uncut forests. Washington's first sawmill was built by Tannahill and Lavendar in 1831, on the northern bank of the Tar River, west of where U.S. 17 crosses the Pamlico River. In the 1800s, the Tar River was several feet deep, and large shallow draft flats and scows could be towed west by slaves to the markets of Tarboro. Each scow carried 70 or 80 hogsheads of tobacco or bales of cotton. Since roads were virtually non-existent, waterways were the only way to transport lumber and heavy cargo. The carriage trade on the Old Post Road (the only useable road), from Edenton to New Bern and Wilmington, also increased business, for Washington had become the seat of Beaufort County. This brought many businessmen and visitors to town who sought food and lodging during their stay. As the county seat and an official shipping clearing house, Washington became the central port for exporting the region's production of tar, resin, pitch, turpentine, rosin, corn, boards, scantling, staves, shingles, furs, tobacco, rum, pork, lard, tallow, beeswax, myrtlewax, soya beans, peas, and cabbage.

Washington 1890. By 1890, there were several major lumber mills located on the Washington waterfront: Kugler and Son Lumber, Pamlico Cooperage Co., Havens Mill, Moss Planing Mill Co., Fowle Mill (located on the south side of the Pamlico, east of the old ferry slip), E.M. Short Lumber Co., and Eureka Lumber Co. (west of U.S. 17). There were also several shipbuilders: William Farrow, John Myers, Abner P. Neal, Hull Anderson (a free African American), Jonathan Havens, William L. Lavender. Backing up this industry, on First Street (now Main Street), were dozens of wholesale and retail stores. The mills had located on the water's edge because the river offered the only mode of long-distance transport available until the railroads came through between 1904 and 1909. The Atlantic Coast Line Railroad put in a warehouse and a depot on Gladden Street in 1904. The Washington and Vandemere Railroad arrived in 1905 (west of U.S. 17), and it serviced Eureka Lumber Co. This line ran from Washington to Aurora and Vandemere to the southeast. The Norfolk & Southern Railroad Line (NSR) laid tracks and a swing-bridge (with a cupola watch tower) between the north and south shores of the Pamlico River in 1909. This NSR line crossed the river just east of Castle Island and ended in Chocowinity. Freight trains still run this route daily from Chocowinity through Havens Garden (the site of the old Pamlico Cooperage Co.) in Washington. The sailing ships began to disappear soon after, for it was quicker and cheaper to ship by rail. A period of inflation occurred after World War I, followed by a recession in the mid-1920s and the devastating 1929 Wall Street crash. By the early 1930s, the nation was in the grasp of a great depression, and so was Washington. In Washington, several WPA and CCA projects helped some, but World War II took away much young manpower. By the early 1940s, most of the lumber mills had closed.

Washington 2000. While Washington's economy has had its ebbs and flows, the city is on the rise again. The entire downtown business district has been renovated, along with the waterfront and beautiful Stewart Parkway. Many new technical jobs have been created in the last ten years, thanks in large measure to the training being offered by Beaufort County Community College.

Washington has only a handful of antebellum homes that precede 1800. Most of the early- to middle-nineteenth-century homes were burned in 1864 by retreating Union troops and again by the disastrous fire of 1900. Most of the brick commercial buildings in downtown's Historic Business District were built after the 1900 fire, which burned down all of Water Street and all of Market Street north one block to Main Street. This fire spurred the City of Washington to change its fire code to require all commercial buildings to be built of brick.

Visitors will, however, find a fine array of mid-to-late 1800s and early 1900s homes and commercial buildings of revival, colonial, Greek, traditional cottages, and various other architectural styles worth viewing. Because it is the county seat, Washington is once again growing and retains an important position in the economy of Eastern North Carolina. Washington, like most of Northeastern North Carolina, enjoys a mild climate, a modest tax rate, and a friendly atmosphere, all of which make this area very desirable for retirement. The Pamlico River, though no longer a commercial shipping lane, offers unlimited recreational opportunities for boating and fishing. The city renewed its interest in historic preservation under the leadership of Mayor Thomas Stewart during the 1960s. Work is constantly in progress to preserve and renew historic homes and Main Street and Market Street buildings. Outstanding leadership is coming forth from the Washington Area Historic Foundation, the Washington Beaufort County Chamber of Commerce, and the Washington Historic District Merchants Association. The City of Washington steadfastly lives up to its motto: "Pride in the past, faith in the future."

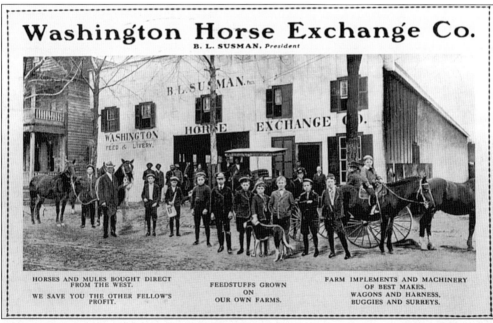

In 1913, B.L. Susman advertised his Washington Horse Exchange Co. in a sales booklet called *Washington, North Carolina*. The author and photographer are unknown, but it was printed by the Press of Joseph J. Stone & Company of Greensboro, North Carolina, for the Washington Chamber of Commerce. The author proclaimed that "If there be one city in the old North State which affords more fruitful interest to the capitalist, the manufacturer or the home seeker, than another, that city is Washington. . . . [for] nowhere in the South has this writer found a greater abundance of milk of human kindness, or a higher regard for the personal care of their fellowman, than pervades the city of Washington, North Carolina." (WL.)

One

THE WASHINGTON WATERFRONT

1800s–1969

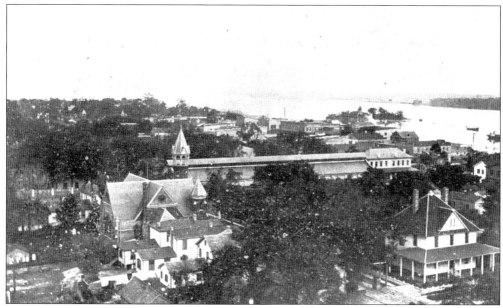

This bird's-eye view of Washington, looking southeast in 1905, was taken from the water tower. The Russian-style bell tower of the First United Methodist Church is prominent on Second Street. Behind it, on Gladden Street, is the Atlantic Coast Line Railroad's warehouse building with its depot at the far end. The large home at the bottom right was the Frank A. Moss home on Van Norden Street, built in 1890. This house has been converted into a bed and breakfast by Leonard and Johanna Huber. (PC OS.)

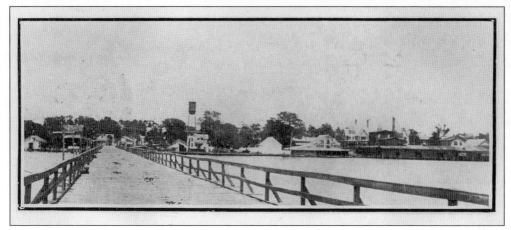

This picture from the wooden "Tar River Bridge" (now the U.S. 17 Pamlico River Bridge), looking north, was taken about 1895 (Yes, those are horse droppings.). At the far end is a steel object, which is a swing-bridge. However, the very first wooden bridge across the river was built about 1799 and was operated by Bryan Grimes as a toll road until 1879, when the State bought it from him for $4,500. Grimes charged a nickel per person toll for crossing and 50¢ for a four-wheeled vehicle. At that time, the road was part of the Colonial Highway, which was cleared in 1722 from Edenton through Bath and across the Tar River Bridge to New Bern. (PC OS.)

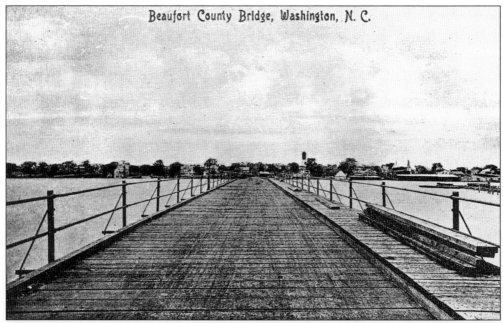

This view looks north along the "Beaufort County Bridge" (Pamlico River Bridge) in 1908. This bridge replaced the Tar River Bridge lost in the 1898 Hurricane. The new bridge was wider and had a walkway and steel rail posts. On the right side, at the north end of the bridge, is the bridge tender's house, which is attached to the bridge. On the left side are the Government Buoy Yard, the water tower (from where the bird's-eye view was taken [seen on page 9]), Havens Wharf and Havens docks, the Fowle & Son warehouse docks, the Presbyterian Church steeple (in background). (PC OS.)

10

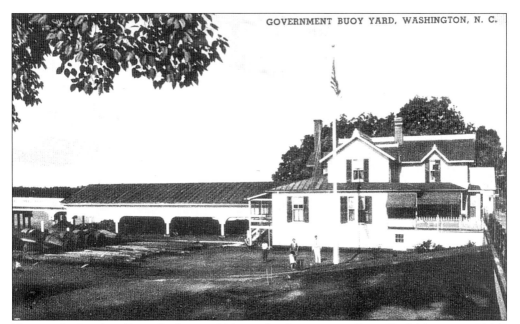

Next to the Pamlico River Bridge in 1920 was the Government Buoy Yard (shown c. 1920s), which faced First Street (now Main Street). Channel buoys were scraped, painted, and returned to their channel positions by buoy tenders (see *Holly* below). The USO Recreation Center moved next door from East Second Street in January 1942. (PC WM.)

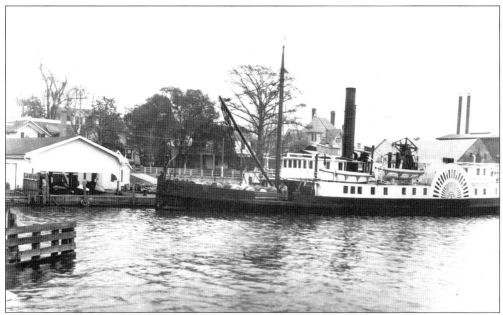

The streamlined side-wheel steamer Buoy Tender *Holly* is docked at the Government Buoy Yard pier. It was "the last side-wheeler to sail on the Pamlico," said native Henry B. Rumley. She was replaced by the *Maple* on February 20, 1931. The Fowle House can be seen beyond the Pilot House. Havens Wharf is off the stern. (HR.)

11

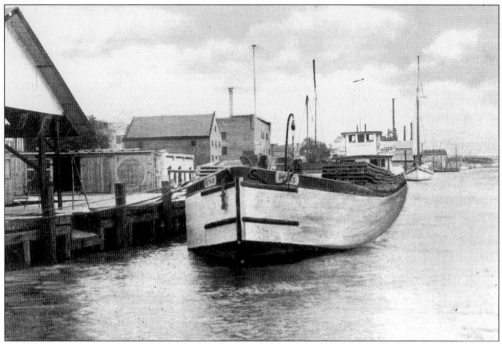

This barge, *Buoys,* is moored at the ACL Railroad Wharf. These barges were also used to transport bales of cotton and tobacco up the Tar River to market in Tarboro in the 1800s. In the background is Havens Wharf and Havens Oil Co. Directly behind the barge is a Chesapeake Bay Skipjack. (PC OS.)

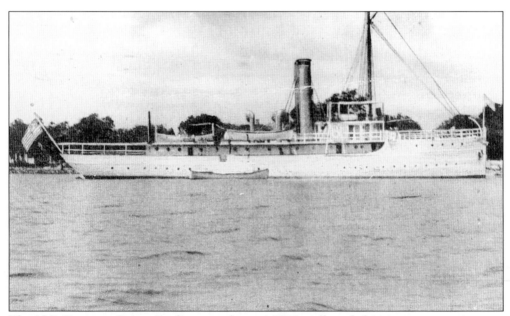

The U.S. Revenue Cutter *Pamlico,* seen here *c.* 1900, collected shipping taxes on imports, mainly from the West Indies ships, until 1942, when she was refitted as a WWII mine sweeper. The *Pamlico* visited all of the major ports of Eastern North Carolina. (PC OS.)

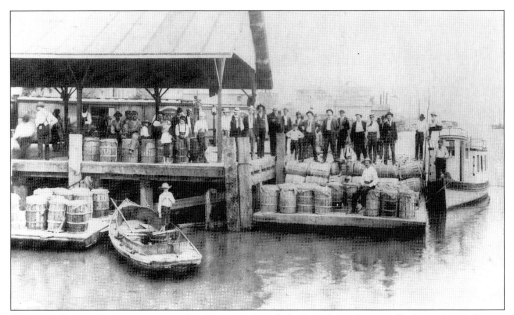

In 1906, Styron Transportation Co. had a railroad dock only a short walk from the Atlantic Coast Line train depot. Barrels of Irish potatoes grown on J.E. Clarke's plantation near Tranters Creek await loading for shipment. Also of interest, the "Grandest Excursion of the season," which traveled to Ocracoke Island aboard the side-wheeler *Aurora*, departed from this dock on Saturdays at 6 a.m. and returned from Ocracoke at 6 p.m. on Sunday, reaching Washington at 1 a.m. on Monday. The round-trip fare was $2, and children under 12 were charged half price. W.T. Farrow was the agent. (DM.)

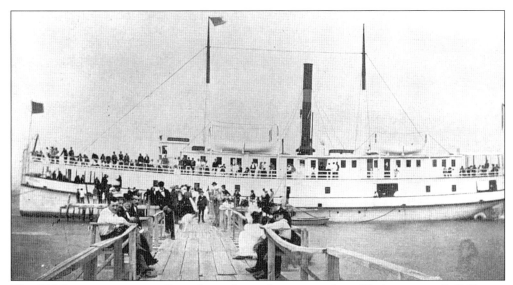

The Old Dominion steamer *Ocracoke* made regular voyages from Washington to Bell Haven, and on to Ocracoke Island. Ocracoke had three fine hotels and several boardinghouses that served excellent seafood. Guests could swim and fish during the day and square dance at night. (OS.)

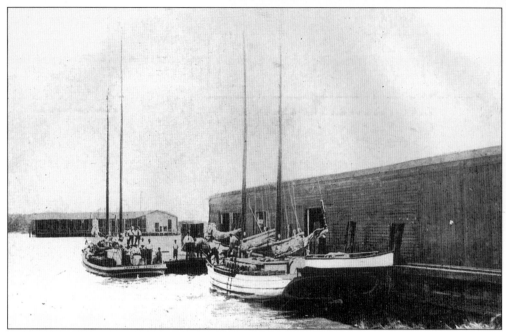

The Havens warehouse docks were built around 1890, and they extended well out into the river so that these shallow-draft Chesapeake Bay schooners could dock to load and unload cargo. The schooner in the foreground has been loaded with barrels of Beaufort County Irish potatoes bound for Northern markets. (PC OS.)

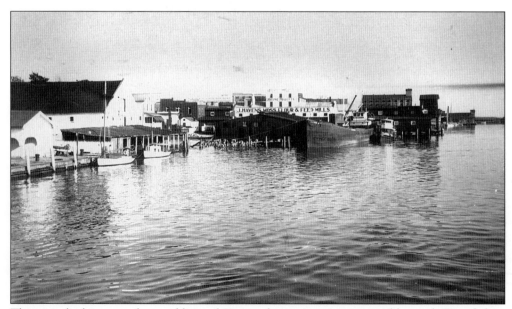

This view looking east shows additional Havens business enterprises and beyond. From left to right, they are as follows: the Government Buoy Yard, Havens Warehouse, the J. Havens Flour and Feed Mill, Havens Grist Mill, Pamlico Chemical Co., and Phillips Fertilizer Co. (HR.)

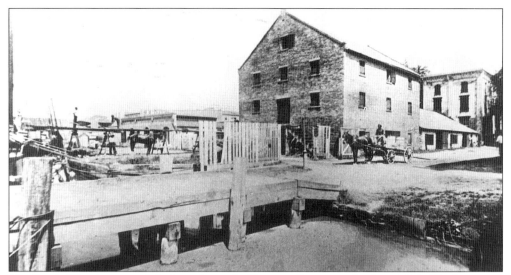

The Fowle Warehouse and dock at the end of Respess Street was built in 1825. The basement and foundation were built with ballast rocks. Fowle ships loaded naval stores and merchandise bound for New England and the West Indies. The Fowle brothers built a sawmill and a shipyard on Castle Island from 1818 through 1887. Carter, Archie & Hassel restored the Fowle warehouse in 1984 and fitted it out for their law offices. The 201 West Main Street Fowle & Son store became the Curiosity Shoppe Cafe & Bar in the late 1990s. (BRL.)

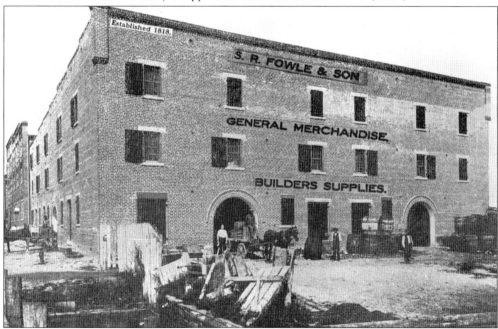

S.R. Fowle, a commission merchant, built this General Merchandise warehouse across from his other Respess Street warehouse and dock around 1903. It had storefronts on Main Street, where Fowle & Son sold builder's supplies: lime, cement and plaster of Paris, general merchandise, sash, doors, window glass, paints, oil, spirits, and turpentine. In the late 1990s, these storefronts were being occupied by Washington Jewelry (est. 1962), Collen Lupton Insurance Agency, and Mar-Lo's Flowers. (WL.)

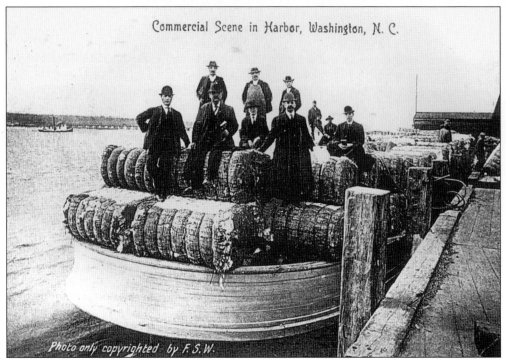

This 1908 "Commercial Scene in Harbor" shows a large open barge loaded with 70 to 80 bales of cotton ready to be towed up the Tar River by tugboat to market in Tarboro. The proud-looking men on board were probably cotton growers. (BRL.)

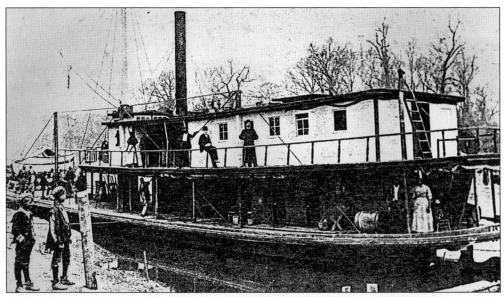

In 1907, the river steamer *R.L. Myers* was under the command of Captain William Parvin, who was one of the original members of the Washington Grays in 1861. The *Myers*'s shipyard was located between Bonner and Harvey Streets. Moonlight excursions were then popular as charity raisers for local churches. The *Myers* carried 50 passengers, with an adult fare of 50¢, and a child fare of 25¢. Ice cream was 5¢ and 10¢ a saucer, and cake was 5¢ a slice. (BRL.)

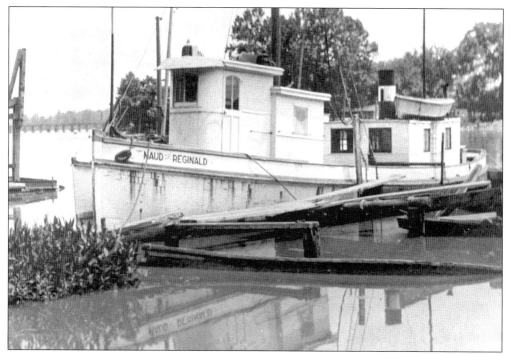

The *Maud & Reginald* was a 60-foot "buy" boat owned and operated by the Swindell-Fulford Fish Co. from 1916 until 1933. Captain John Wesley Dudley, with Archie Dowdy as crew, would "buy" ice from Crystal Ice Co., located next door on Water Street. The *Maud* would sell block ice and fish in ports along the Pamlico. Returning home, Captain Dudley would "buy" catches from local fishermen, ice the fish down, and return to Water Street. (HR.)

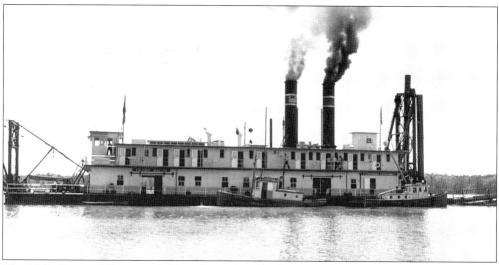

The U.S. Corps of Engineers' 36-inch pipeline dredge *Henry Bacon* is working the shipping channel in the Pamlico River. From 1890 until about 1950, the main shipping channel was dredged to a depth of 20 feet; deep-channel dredging then ceased, and big ships no longer came to Washington. Lumber was shipped by rail, and cotton and tobacco went by truck. By 1950, only fishing boats and pleasure craft plied the Pamlico River. (HR.)

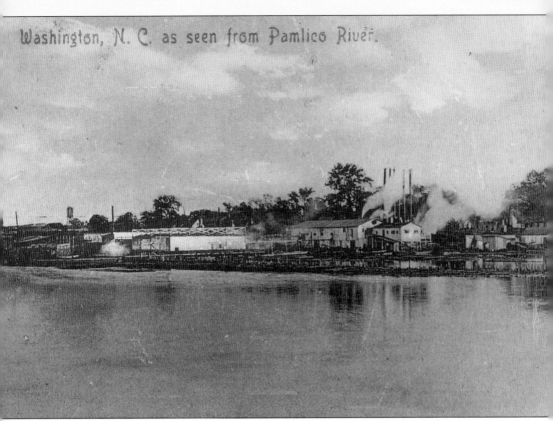

This Pamlico River waterfront scene, taken from Castle Island in 1911, shows, from left to right, the T.H.B. Myers Shipyard (est. 1884), the Moss Planing Mill (white buildings), and the Kugler Lumber Company (est. 1881), which extended east from the foot of Harvey Street. (PC OS.)

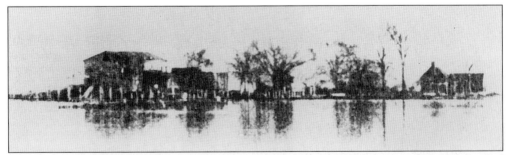

This view captures Castle Island around 1905. In the early 1800s, Josiah, Sam, Luke, James, and Luther Fowle arrived in Washington, and they operated a sawmill and a shipbuilding business on Castle Island from 1818 until 1887, when they sold out the business to Clarance Branning. During the Civil War, Union troops built a fortification here. In 1902, Doc Bryan had a fishery there and caught and processed millions of herring. He gave away the fish roe because he had no way of canning or freezing the roe. Later on, there was a kiln built to burn leftover oyster shells. The kiln funnels looked like the turrets on a castle, so they called the island "the Castle." (CC.)

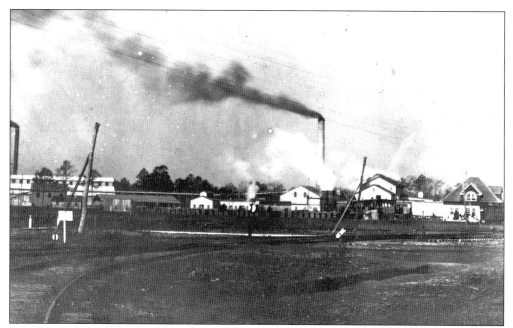

Seen here in 1912, the Pamlico Cooperage Co., located on the Havens Gardens site, evolved from the old Moore Lumber Company. In the foreground are the tracks of the Norfolk Southern and their depot, on the right. The NSR crossed the Pamlico River just east of Castle Island and ended in Chocowinity. (PC OS.)

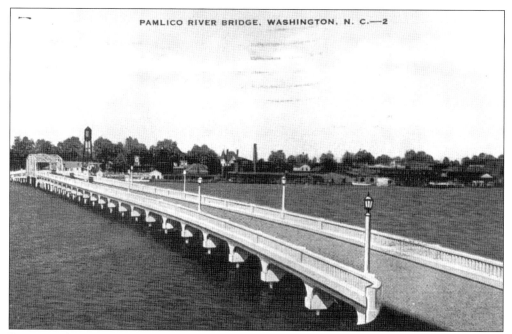

By 1920, the Pamlico River Bridge was paved and had a concrete walkway on both sides, and the swing-bridge cupola had been removed. The smoke stack belongs to the Washington Laundry structure, built about 1915, which later became the Capehart-Brown Laundry. (PC OS.)

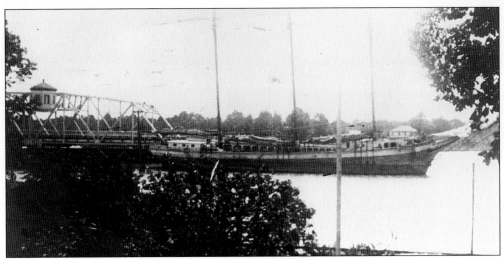

The three-masted schooner *Ram*, built in 1900, comes through the Pamlico River swing-bridge on her way up the Tar River to the Eureka Lumber Co. for a load of lumber to deliver to Norfolk, Baltimore, and Philadelphia. The *Ram* had unloaded her inbound cargo of fertilizer and hardware for the Harris Hardware Co. at their Water Street dock. "Harris Hardware had seven traveling salesmen covering territory from Virginia to South Carolina, and west as far as Durham," said Washington native Henry B. Rumley. (HR.)

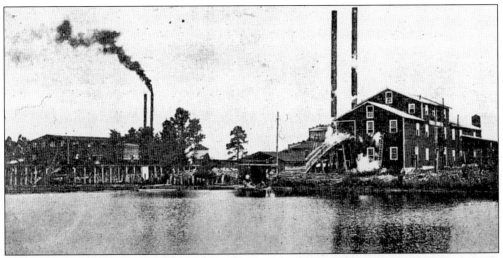

The Eureka Lumber Co., c. 1894, was the largest sawmill operation in Washington at the turn of the century. Owned by George T. Leach, George A. Phillips, and W.T. Campen, Eureka produced wooden mine props, rollers, and lumber. Leach also owned part of the Pamlico Cooperage Co. (Havens Garden site) and Paragon Lumber Co. in Bath. Pamlico Cooperage produced potato barrels, bean baskets, and beet crates. Eureka burned down in 1911 and again in 1951; each time it was quickly rebuilt. Eureka could only import tree lumber by barge, so in 1905, Leach organized the Vandermere Railroad, which gave Eureka a rail facility that could import virgin timberland from southeastern Beaufort County. Weyerhaeuser purchased Eureka in 1956 and closed the plant three months later. Henry Griffin of Williamston purchased the idle mill in 1958. By 1975, most of the remaining machinery was sold to a mill in Gassaway, West Virginia. (PC OS.)

Two

THE WASHINGTON
WATERFRONT
1969–1999

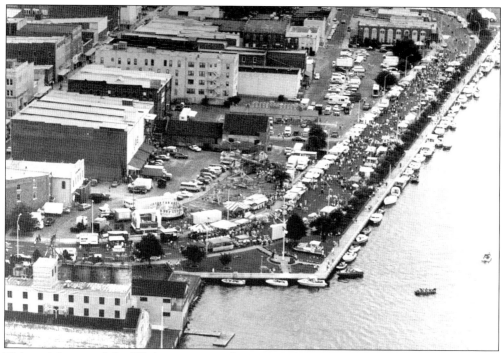

This aerial view of the Washington waterfront was taken during the 1990 Summer Festival. Washington residents and friends enjoy the fun and the beauty of the Pamlico River. All the old warehouses, except the Havens and Fowle warehouses have been torn down and replaced by Stewart Parkway. However, most of the Main and Water Streets commercial buildings and the J. Havens Moss grainery (lower left) remain. (AR; courtesy BL.)

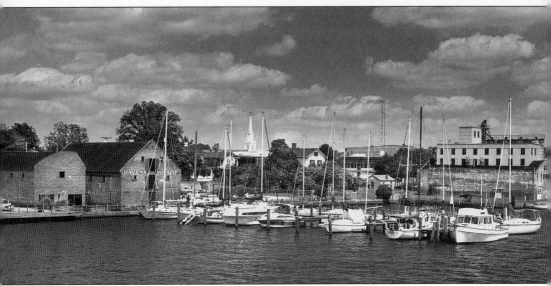

Since 1990, this scene greeted visitors and residents from the Pamlico River Bridge; from left to right, they are Havens Wharf and annex (added to left side in 1988) and Havens-Moss gristmill (background). The 1900s dock had been replaced with boat slips by Carolina Wind Yachting Center Inc. (VC.)

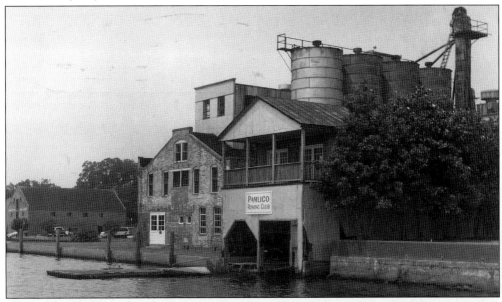

This view shows the Havens-Moss gristmill, built c. 1830 and located on southside 300 block on West Main Street. Jonathan Havens was a commission merchant and dealer in corn and meal, hay and oats, cotton seed meal, hulls and coal. "The mill is a magnificent structure, modern in its equipment throughout, and the products are unrivaled for purity, strength, freshness, color and uniformity," said a review in a Washington, North Carolina journal in 1915. During the Depression, a grain bank was operated here for the benefit of farmers. The mill is no longer in use, but the majority of the machinery still operates. The Pamlico Rowing Club of Raleigh no longer uses the water shed. The Havens Wharf building can be seen to the left. (VC.)

22

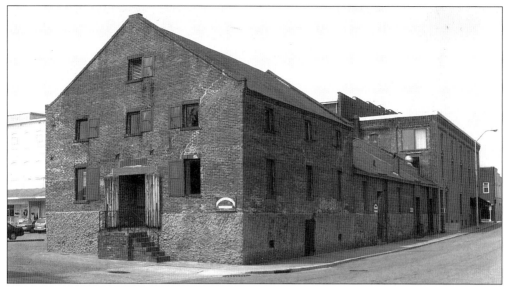

The Fowle warehouse, built c. 1840, was constructed at 112 Respess Street. The basement and foundation were built from ballast stone from the bilges of West Indies trading vessels. Blacks from the West Indies, wearing bright bandannas and large golden rings in their ears, would unload hogsheads of molasses, much to the delight of Washington's girls and boys! The bouncing from unloading caused the molasses to foam, making it necessary to knock the bung from the hole. The leaking golden brown foam was caught in little tin buckets by the children. That night, the children had a molasses taffy pull. (VC.)

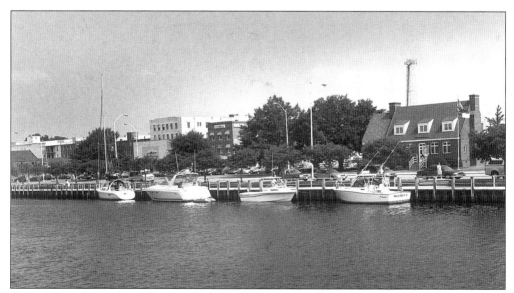

Here, boats dock along Stewart Parkway waterfront bulkhead. The Washington Beaufort County Chamber of Commerce building, a replica of the Newbold White House in Hertford, is visible on the right. The City of Washington offers overnight curbside electric hookups for boaters and RVs. (VC.)

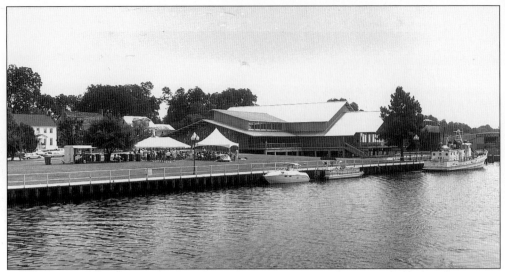

On August 21, 1999, the Washington/Greenville Power Squadron held a water safety class in a tent on the front lawn of the North Carolina Estuarium. All of the river scenes shown in Chapter Two were taken from the fly bridge of Jerry Hannon's 37-foot Silverton. (VC.)

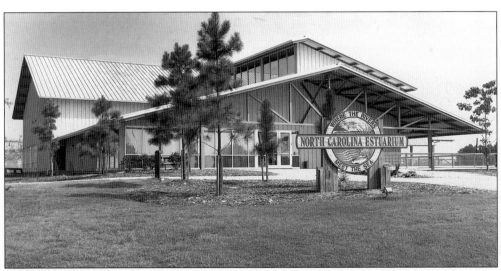

The North Carolina Estuarium is located at 223 East Water Street, overlooking the beautiful Pamlico River, "Where the Rivers Meet the Sea." The estuarium combines environmental displays with a unique blend of art and science. There are over 200 exhibits and historic artifacts on display. (VC.)

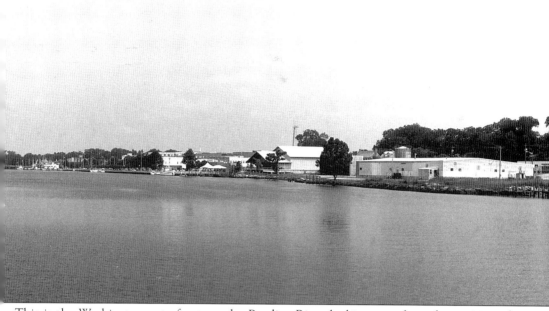

This is the Washington waterfront on the Pamlico River looking west from the position of Castle Island (seen on page 18). The Moss Building Supply, Inc. is the one-story white building, which is the approximate site of the large Kugler Lumber Co., established in 1881. To the left of Moss Brothers Lumber Co. is the North Carolina Estuarium, formerly the location of T.H.B. Myers Shipyard (1895) and Chauncey's Ways Boatyard (1900), which later became Wilder Shipyard, until it closed in 1938. (VC.)

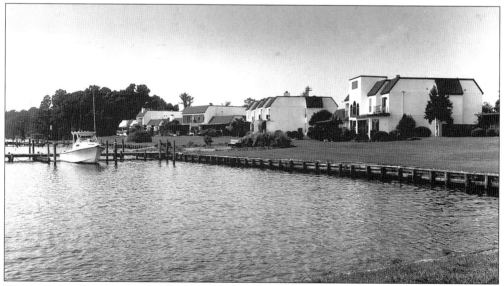

On the west side of U.S. 17, where the Tar River meets the Pamlico, is Washington Harbour. This community was developed by Jack H. Brazier on the site of the Eureka Lumber Mill. The mill ceased operating in 1956, when it was bought by the North Carolina Pulp Co. (now Weyerhaeuser), and it closed three months later. (VC.)

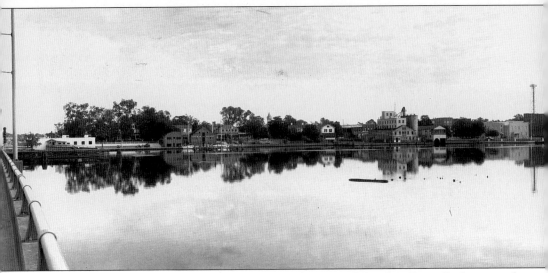

This Pamlico River panorama looking east from the U.S. 17 Pamlico River Bridge was taken shortly after Hurricane Floyd devastated Eastern North Carolina. On the left stands Snookies Restaurant, where the 1890 Government Buoy Yard was located, and to its right are the 1820 Havens Wharf building and the 1990 annex building, which were damaged and are presently being restored. The 1890 Haven-Moss Feed Grainery survived. The original 1900s docks were demolished in the late 1960s when Stewart Parkway was built. (VC.)

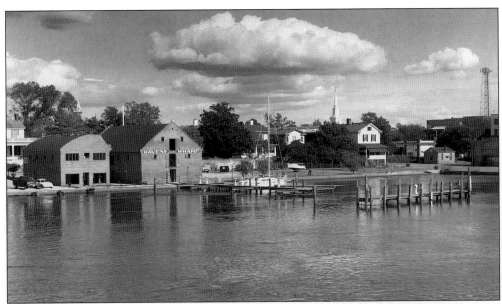

In late 1999, the Havens Wharf scene (page 22) changed dramatically. Hurricane Floyd caused the river to rise almost 7 feet, which inundated Havens Wharf and annex and destroyed most of the Carolina Wind Yachting Center boat slips. Owner Cliff Furlough's office reported that the buildings and slips will be repaired as soon as possible. (VC.)

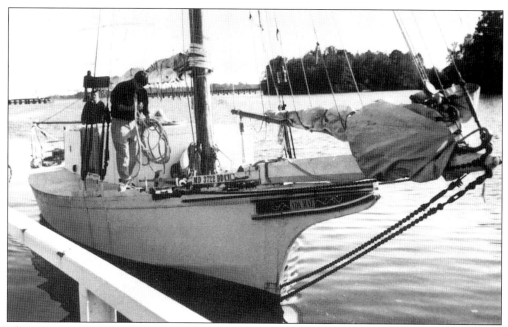

The Chesapeake skipjack *Ada Mae* docks at the North Carolina Estuarium in Washington in November 1996, after sailing from Norfolk, Virginia. Ada Mae Hodges was the youngest sister of Captain Ralph B. Hodges, who built the skipjack in 1915 in Rose Bay, Hyde County. Captain Hodges named his skipjack in her honor. Student David Smith of Eastern Carolina University (ECU) gathers a line, while helmsman ECU professor Gordon Watts guides the *Ada Mae* while docking. The *Ada Mae* is being restored at McCotters Marina in Washington. (KS and ZH.)

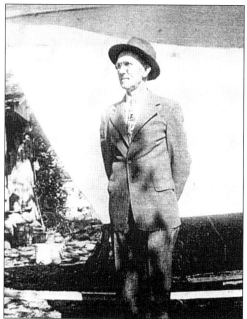
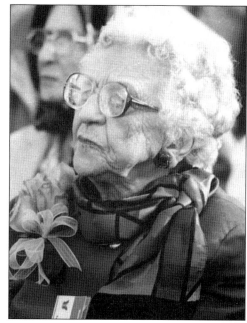

Left: This is a portrait of Captain Ralph B. Hodges. *Right:* This photograph captures the inspiration for Hodges's skipjack, Ada Mae Hodges Cowan.

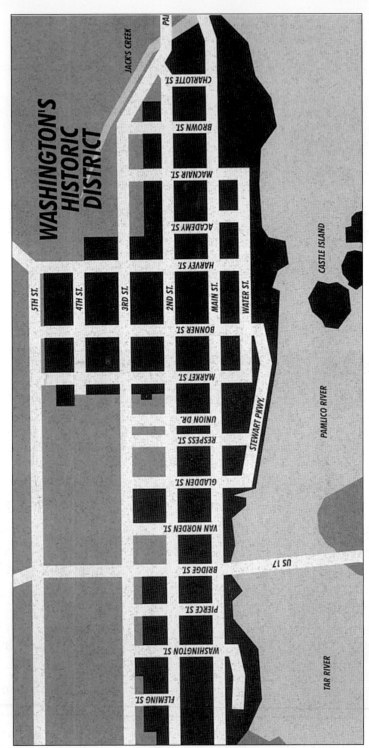

This map shows Washington's Historic District.

Three
THE HISTORIC
BUSINESS DISTRICT
1900–1999

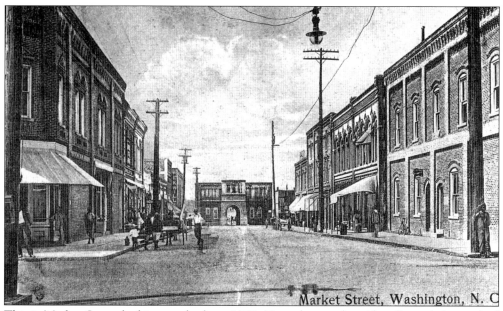

This is Market Street looking south about 1900. Note the wooden sidewalks and the crushed oyster shell street. The building at the end of Market Street was called the "Market." Designed and built of wood by Charles Hartge around 1895, the Market was the home of the Armory, which burned in 1900, when a fire gutted Water Street and both sides of Market Street up to Main Street. As a result of this fire, the city building code for commercial structures was changed from wood to brick. The Market was rebuilt of brick in 1901. Jack's Furniture was on the left, with Leonard's Hardware across the street on the northeast corner. Behind the Market was the Meyers warehouse and dock, where the Old Dominion Steamship Line operated. (PC OS.)

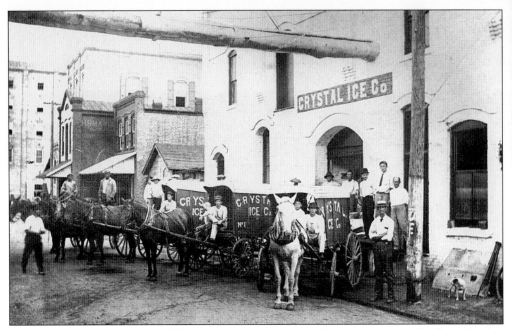

The Crystal Ice Co., which sold block ice, was located on Water Street near Dudley's Market in 1912. Maola Ice Cream, a Sunday favorite of many Washington families, was next door. Crystal Ice Co. later became Colonial Ice Co., which was demolished in 1960 after flood inundation. (AF.)

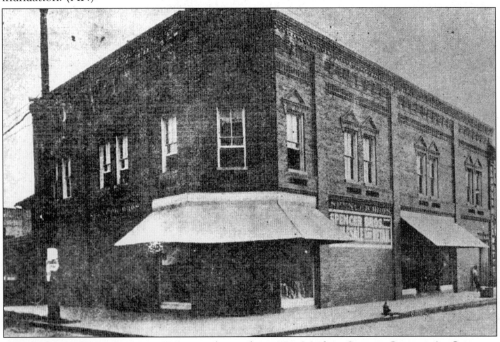

The Spencer Bros. Co., c. 1895, was located at 101 Market Street. George A. Spencer, proprietor, sold dry goods, notions, clothes, and shoes. They were complete outfitters for the whole family. Whatever the fashion was in New York, you were soon to find it at Spencer Bros. Wachovia Bank built on this corner in 1968. (IN.)

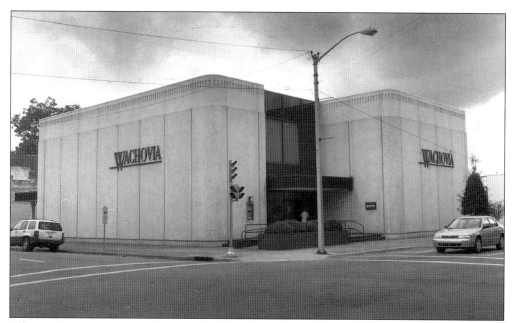

White's Store occupied the Spencer building from about 1920 to 1930. Then, Guarantee Bank used it for many years. The Spencer building was demolished in 1968, when Wachovia Bank built on this corner. (VC.)

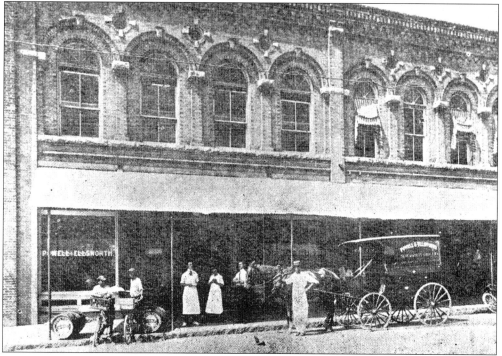

Powell & Ellsworth constructed this building, with a basement, at 120 South Market Street in 1913. The owners were Messrs. W.T. Powell and W.H. Ellsworth. They specialized in "quality groceries." A horse-drawn wagon was used for home deliveries, and two delivery boys with bicycles served local addresses.

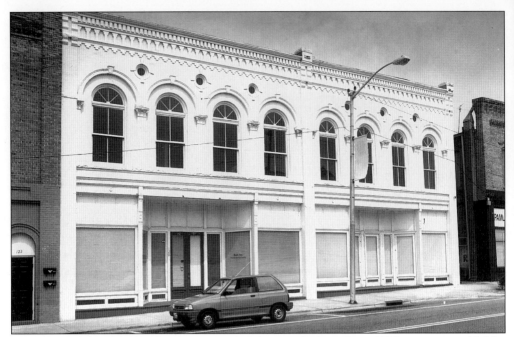

The Ellsworth building has been renovated and painted white. Late-1990s tenants are Nobles & Keech, P.A., and Hoell Inc. (VC.)

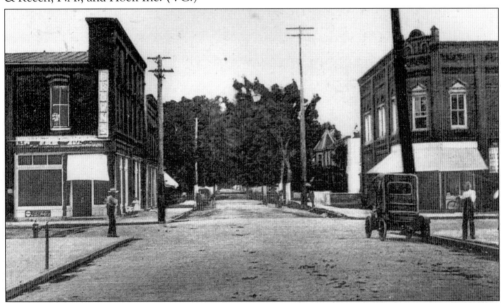

This is Main Street looking east in 1909. Main Street is now paved with brick. On the left side was the Brown building, where Brown's Drugstore (first floor) and Brown's Opera House (second floor) were located. The next building was the Fulford Hardware Co., situated there from 1885 to 1907, when the Ellison Brothers Co. moved in. Next door (which is now a parking lot) was the Dimock house, where pioneer Susan Dimock, M.D., was born. Ms. Dimock was the first North Carolina woman to become a doctor in 1871. Dimock drowned while returning home when the steamship *Shiller* sank in 1875; she was only 26 years of age. Then came the Patrician Inn. On the right corner was Spencer's Grocery Store. (PC OS.)

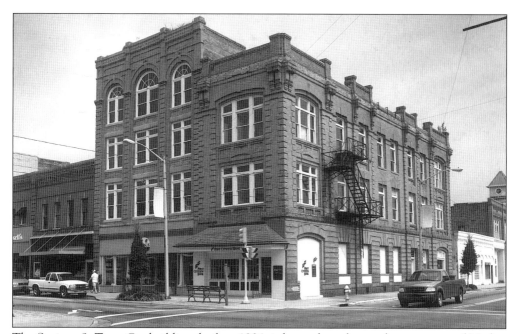

The Savings & Trust Co. building, built *c.* 1904, is located on the northwest corner of Market and Main Streets. This handsome three-story brick commercial building has wide arched openings, corbeled trim, an ornamental parapet, and various classical details. Beverly Moss was president of the Savings & Trust Bank, and J.B. Sparrow was cashier. Two years later, the Home Building and Loan also had offices here, and J.B. Sparrow served as the secretary. First Citizen's Bank was located here until late 1999. (VC.)

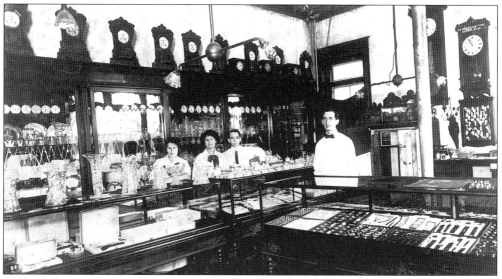

Stewart's Jewelry Store, located at 121 North Market Street, first opened in 1910. "Every week for 75 years, one of the family members climbed the narrow courthouse stairs (now BHM Library) to the garret to undertake the tedious process of winding the town clock's heavy striking and running weights that struck every hour and half hour," said Thomas Stewart. Stewart Parkway, on the Pamlico River waterfront, was named after former Mayor Thomas A. Stewart on June 15, 1970. (TS.)

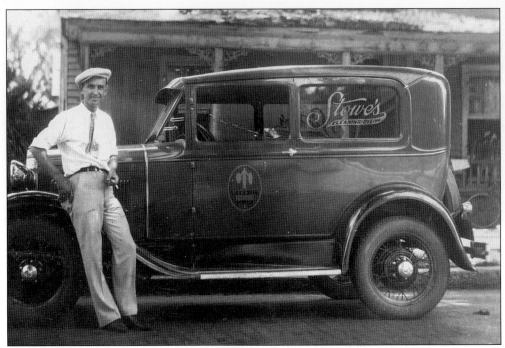

Guy and Ben Stowe opened their dry cleaning store at 116 North Market Street around 1924 and closed in 1960. Judge George H. Brown had his law office here around 1900, and Baker's Studio was also located at this site from about 1910 until 1923. (BL.)

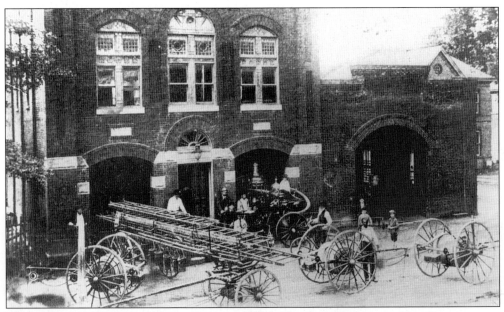

This is Central Station on Market Street, c. 1895. The first Washington Fire Company was formed in 1791. Interestingly, any carter, or drayman, who pulled his fire equipment to and from a fire was paid $1. In 1884, Beaufort County constructed a town hall, which became Central Station on Market Street, to house firefighting equipment, horses, and a jail. (BRL.)

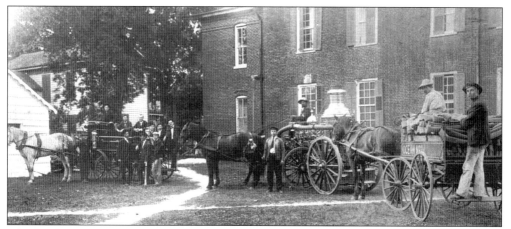

The fire department of 1898 consisted of the following (from left to right): a horse-drawn pump wagon, a horse-drawn steamer, and a horse-drawn hose wagon. (FD.)

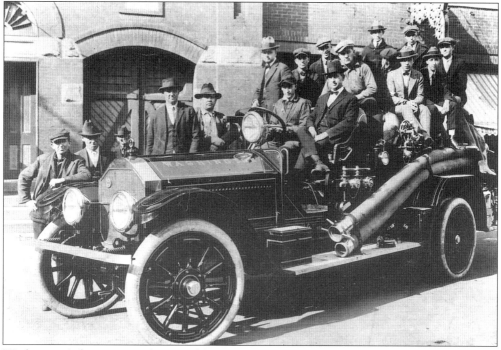

Washington's first motorized piece of fire equipment was a Model 12 American-La France fire truck purchased in 1914 and made operational in 1916. It had right-hand steering, hard rubber tires, and a 6-cylinder, dual ignition, chain-driven gas engine. Seated beside the driver, Dave Hampton, is Chief O.M. Winfield. Directly behind Chief Winfield is Archie Kelly, and to his right is Bob Hodges. Over Hodges's left shoulder is R. Lee Stewart (with hat and sweater), and to the far right, John Johnson is visible. To Johnson's lower right is Fred Moore, and Herber Whitley appears with his hands crossed. On back are the following, from left to right : Frank Wright, Caleb Sterling, Elbert Weston, and Coley Tankard. (HR.)

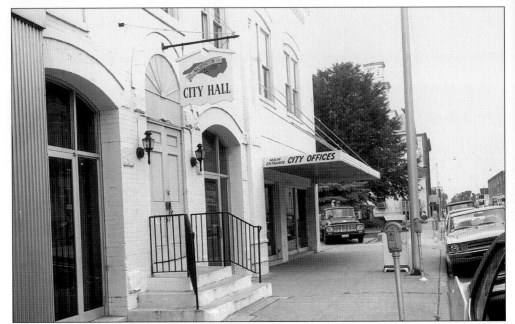

The fire department moved to larger quarters at the corner of Market and Fifth Streets in 1965. Around 1975, the old Central Station building was renovated, painted white, and officially became City Hall, with a second-floor county courtroom. (BRL.)

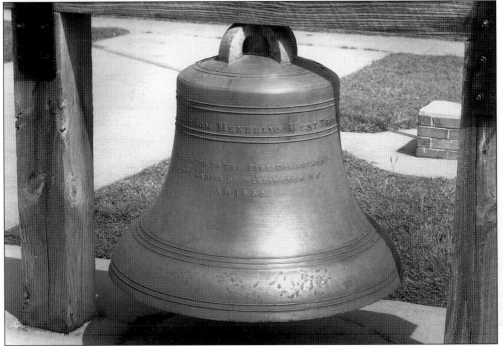

This fine bell hung in the tower of the old fire department's Central Station (old City Hall) until 1965, when it was moved to the present fire department location, at the corner of Fifth and Market Streets, for permanent display. The inscription reads as follows: "Presented to the Fire Department By The Ladies Of Washington, AD 1855." (VC.)

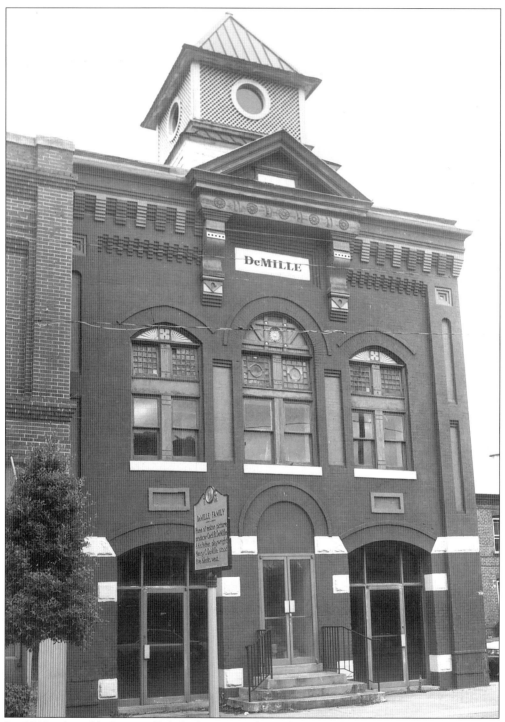

In 2000, the old City Hall (which was to have become the DeMille Museum) stands empty, awaiting funding for another renovation. The Washington Area Historic Foundation wants to restore the old City Hall and is seeking a grant and private donations to complete the project. (VC.)

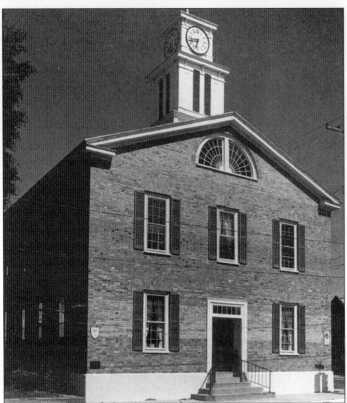

Located at 158 North Market Street, the Beaufort County Courthouse, built c. 1786, is a Federal-era, two-story gable end brick building, laid in Flemish bond with Georgian exterior detail that was restored in 1971, prior to occupation by the BHM Regional Library in 1975. The court moved to the Second Street Courthouse Building in 1974. The original second-floor courtroom is still intact and open for public viewing. (VC.)

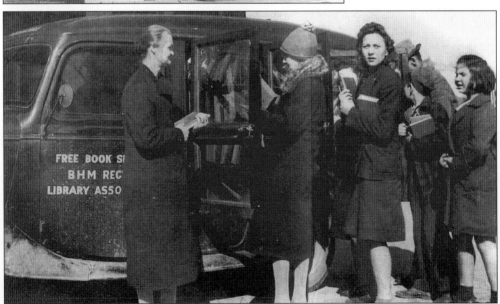

The BHM Regional Library Bookmobile service made its first run in 1941 in this old car nicknamed "Shasta," meaning "she has to go." This "free" book delivery service was organized by Ms. Elizabeth House. In 1999, BHM was operating two modern Bookmobiles that traveled the back roads of Beaufort, Hyde, and Martin Counties, delivering some 4,000 books to residents each month. (BHM.)

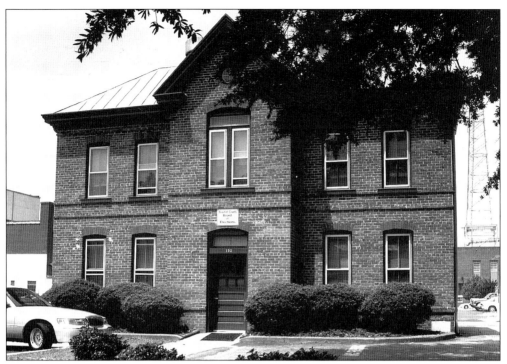

Located at 132 North Market Street, the Board of Elections Building, built *c.* 1890, was the county jail until 1974, when it was relocated to the basement of the County Courthouse Building on Second Street. Juvenile Probation office, Guardian Ad Litem office, and the County Works program offices are also located here. (VC.)

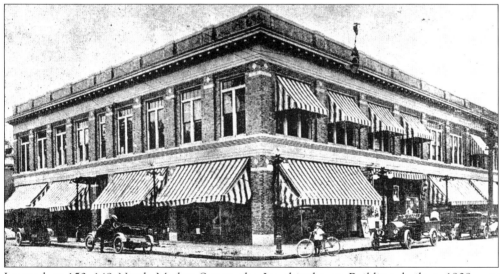

Located at 153–149 North Market Street, the Laughinghouse Building, built *c.* 1908, was constructed by Tom Latham, a well-to-do farmer (Mrs. Laughinghouse's brother). Miss Mollie Vines and Mrs. Wineberg had candy stores in this building; they were the delight of all the children in town. Ed Long's Buggy Factory was also here. (IN.)

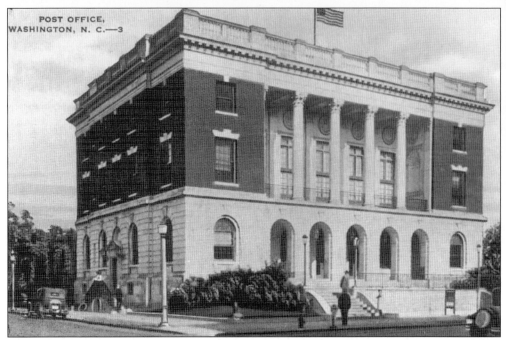

Located at 102 East Second Street, the U.S. Post Office and Federal Courthouse, *c.* 1913, is one of North Carolina's finest early-twentieth-century government buildings. Designed by architect James Knox Taylor, this Beaux Arts Neo-Classical three-story landmark is considered to be the most notable building in town. The Federal Court moved to New Bern in 1978. The post office moved to a new building on the corner of Second and Gladden Streets in 1980. (PC OS.)

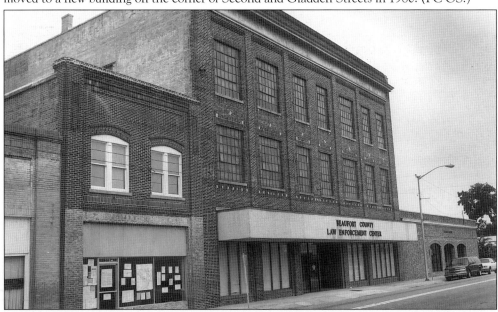

Located at 210 North Market Street, the Okland Building, *c.* 1910, was constructed by Caleb Bell. Bell went in business with Ike Morris, and in 1915, they opened the Belmo Theatre, which closed a year later. In 2000, the Okland Building houses the Beaufort County Law Enforcement Center, which means that it is the sheriff's office. (VC.)

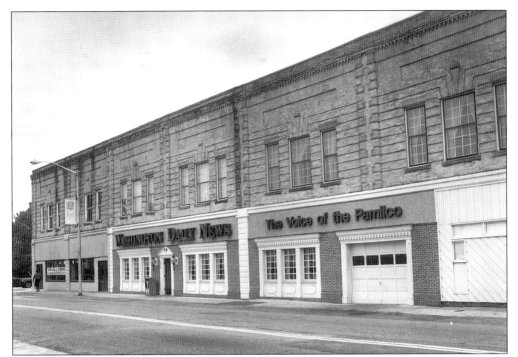

The *Washington Daily News* (*WDN*) became a daily paper in 1909, when James L. Mayo purchased the *Washington Gazette* and changed the name. On November 15, 1949, Ashley B. Futrell purchased *WDN* and adopted the slogan "The Voice of the Pamlico." Ashley Futrell moved *WDN* to its present location at 217 North Market Street in 1953. In 1990, the *WDN* became the smallest daily newspaper to ever win the Pulitzer Prize for public service. (VC.)

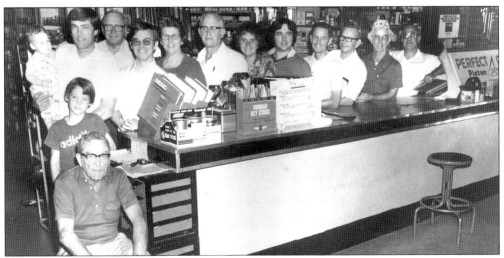

Rumley Motor Supplies, Inc. was in the corner store next to the *Washington Daily News*, where the old Hassel Supply Co. was located in 1910. This 1979 photo shows, from left to right, the following: (seated) Henry B. Rumley Jr.; (behind Rumley) Henry Rumley IV and Henry B. Rumley III (holding Seth C. Rumley); (behind counter) Leonard Nelson, Ronnie Beachham, Anna Mason, R.A. Braddy Jr., Cindy Austin, Gary Lilley, C.B. Mizelle, William R. Jackson, Byron Thomas Jefferson, and Grover Edwards. (HR.)

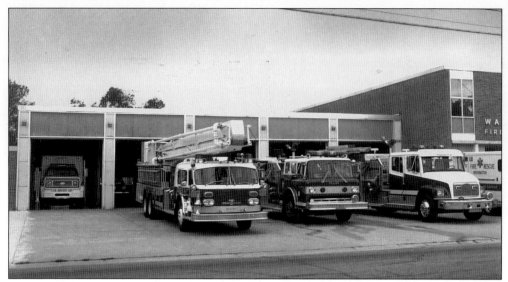

The Washington Fire Department moved to the corner of Fifth and Market Streets in 1965. In 1999, the department had (seen here from left to right) truck 1, hazardous material handler; snorkel 1, an area platform engine; engine 2, used as a second backup engine; engine 1, the main pumper, which can deliver 1,500 g.p.m.; and an EMS rescue medical emergency truck. (VC.)

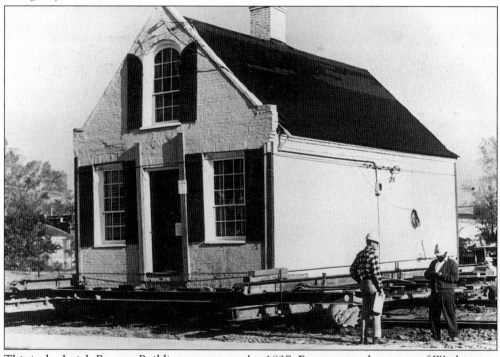

This is the Isaiah Respess Building, constructed c. 1837. Respess was the mayor of Washington in 1862. Washington attorney William Mayo purchased this fine old building and moved it from the middle of Second Street to the corner of Market and Second Streets in 1950. Mayo restored it, added a new wing using the same type and color brick as the original building, and turned it into the Mayo & Mayo Law Office. (WM.)

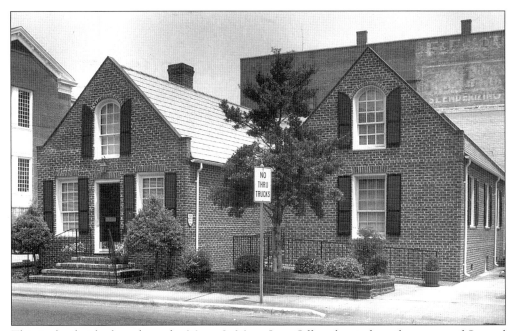

This is the finished product, the Mayo & Mayo Law Office, located on the corner of Second and Market Streets in 1999. (VC.)

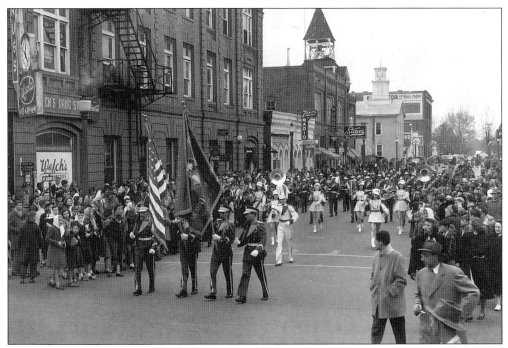

The Washington High School Marching Band is leading a fall parade down Market Street to Main Street in 1948. On the left is Welsh's Drug Store, in the Savings and Trust Co. building, and Stowe's Cleaners (seen on page 34), which was located where Vann's Studio is now. The bell tower of the old City Hall was then an unenclosed structure. (VS.)

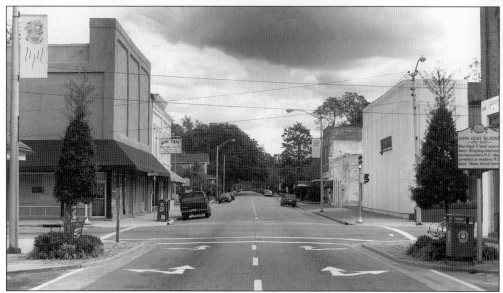

This view shows Main Street looking east from Market Street in 1999. The streets are paved with macadam, instead of brick, and Main Street is one way. The wooden sidewalks have become cement. Attorney Wayland Sermon Jr. is in the old Brown Drug Store at 100 East Main Street, Renn Taff Office Supply is in the old Fulford Hardware Store at 112, and on the southeast corner is the Wachovia Bank, where Spencer Bros. Grocery Store was once located. (VC.)

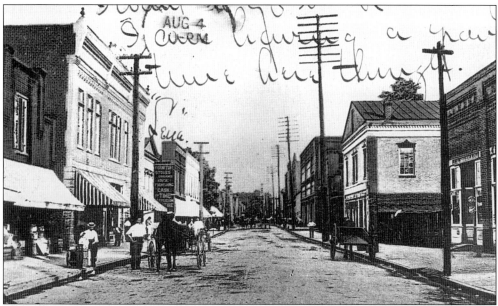

This is Main Street looking east from Gladden Street in 1904. As can be seen in this photograph, Main Street is now paved with brick from Gladden to Market, but the sidewalks may still be made of wood. On the left of the photograph are Ballads Feed Store; W.P. Baugham Building, which had a fertilizer and milling business; and the Bank of Washington. Also visible on the right are the following: S.R. Fowle & Sons store, a vacant lot, and S.R. Wilox & Co. (PC OS.)

Located at 216 West Main Street, the Bank of Washington, established c. 1852, is a Greek Revival temple design bank with tetrastyle Ionic type portico, with stucco-struck exterior made to look like masonry. The founders were E.J. Warren and George H. Brown. (IN.)

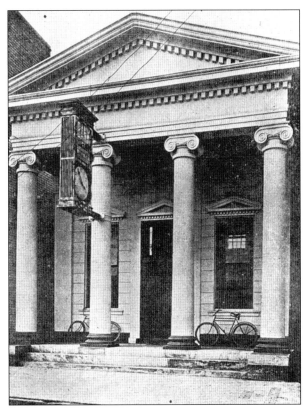

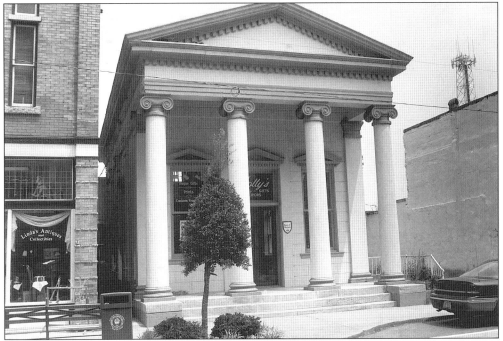

This photo shows the site of the Bank of Washington in 1999. It stands empty as it awaits a new tenant. The magnificent clock that once adorned its facade is now gone. (VC.)

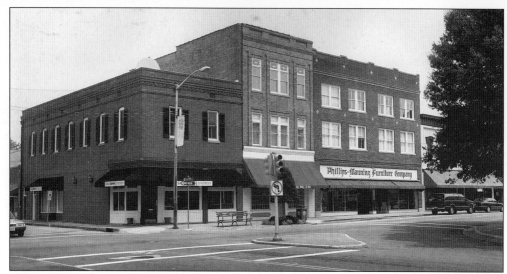

The Rodman building, at 258 West Main Street, was purchased by Lloyd Sloan, restored around 1981, and leased to Edwards & Jones Investments. Ballards Feed Store was located next door (now occupied by an accountant). Phillips-Manning Furniture Company has been in its 246 West Main Street location since 1950. Next is the Talley Building, which Alfred Kelly Millinery and Carter & Taylor Groceries occupied in the early 1900s. William Warren restored the Talley Building in 1981, and he located his Warren's Sport Headquarters at 240 West Main and leased the 238 West Main address to Sunflower Book Store in 1998. (VC.)

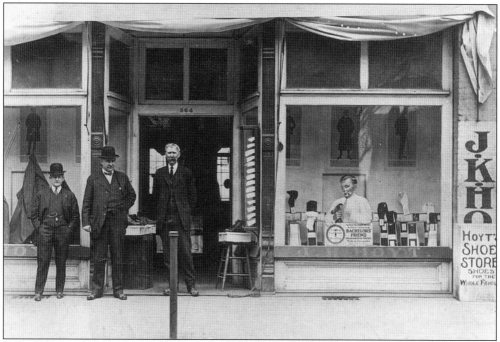

Hoyt's Shoe and Men's Clothing Store, at 204 West Main Street, opened in 1915 and closed in 1924 when he consolidated in his 130 West Main Street store. The proprietors were, from left to right, as follows: John William Isanogle, Charles Hoyt, and C.E. Jordan. Schmitt's Jewelers moved into 204 (now 202) in 1989. (RS.)

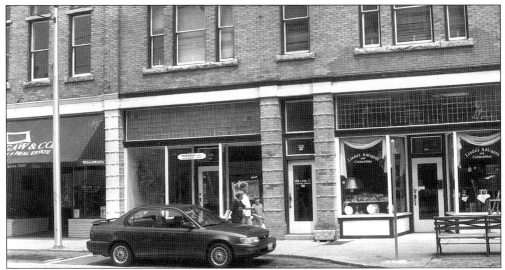

This is the W.P Baughman Building, constructed in 1901 at 218–230 West Main Street. Baugham was a stockholder in five lumber companies. The Elks Club had its headquarters upstairs. Dibble and Associates restored the building in 1980 and now occupy the upstairs. In the late 1990s, Bragaw & Company Insurance & Real Estate occupied 230 West Main, NetSource Computer Systems occupied 228 West Main, and Linda's Antiques and Collectables rented 220 West Main Street. (VC.)

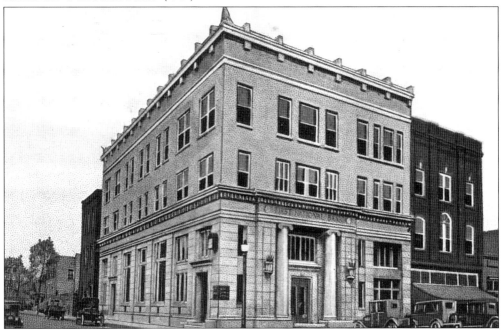

Located at 192 West Main Street, the First National Bank, established *c.* 1916, is a three-story combination stone and brick commercial building. Founded by Dr. Edward Brown as the Beaufort County Bank, it later became the Bank of Washington, then NationsBank, and then Bank of America, which added an ATM in the mid-1990s. Washington's first radio station, WRRF, started in this building on the third floor on March 4, 1942. WRRF's slogan was "We Radiate Real Friendship," the initials of the owners—W.R. Roberson family. (PC OS.)

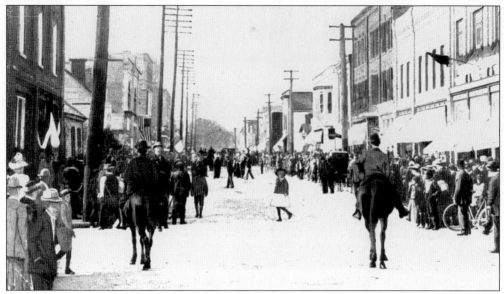

This is Main Street looking west from Market Street in 1900. In 1897, the city commissioners hired the Virginia Brick Paving Co. to brick the streets from Market to Gladden. By 1905, these streets were bricked, and they lasted for 25 years. On the left, the corner building housed the post office and Wynn's Restaurant between 1896 and 1901. The flags flying on Main Street suggest a July 4, 1900 celebration. (PC OS.)

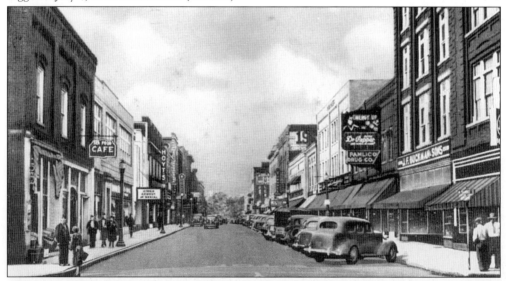

This is Main Street looking west from Market Street in 1937. In this view, Main Street now has two-way traffic, with parking on the north side. On the left, the post office has moved to its own building on the corner of Second and Market Streets in 1915. Wynn's Restaurant is now the Sea Food Cafe. The Reita Theater was next to Hoyt's, followed by the Diamond Cafe; then came Harris Hardware, the McKeel-Richardson Hardware Co., and, on the corner of Union Alley, Walter Credle Co. Visible on the right side are Welch's Drug Store, J.F. Buckman & Sons, Pamlico Drug Co., the Nicholson Hotel, E.W. Ayers Drygoods, Louis and Calais Women's Outfitters, the Turnage Theater, and, on the far corner, Bower Brothers Co. Beside Union Alley is Belk Tyler. (PC OS.)

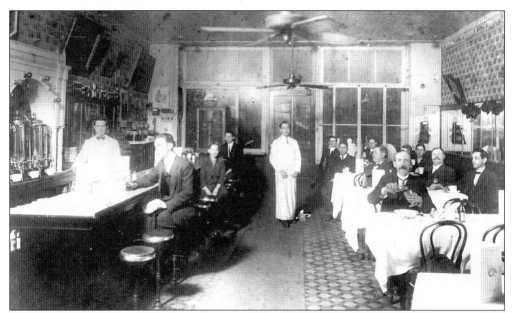

The Diamond Cafe, established *c.* 1910, was located next to Hoyt's on West Main Street. Their slogan was "The Greek Restaurant and Quick Lunch." This 1920s photo shows George Diamond behind the counter and Pete Diamond in the aisle. (HR.)

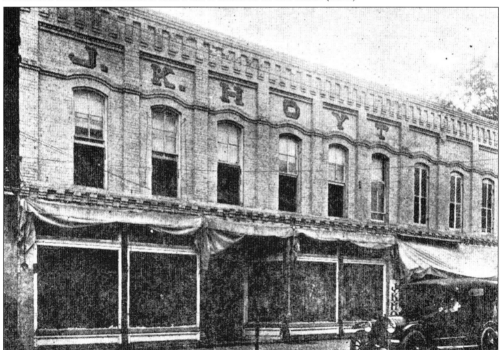

The J.K. Hoyt building on West Main Street was Washington's leading men's and women's fashion center in 1913. Hoyt was the first merchant in town to sell ready-made clothes; they were a sensation. "Miss Pennie Meyers' hats at Hoyt's were the heart's desire of every girl in Washington," said Mrs. Pattie Baugham McMullen of Washington Park. Tassel's Gift Shop occupied the store in the late 1990s. (IN.)

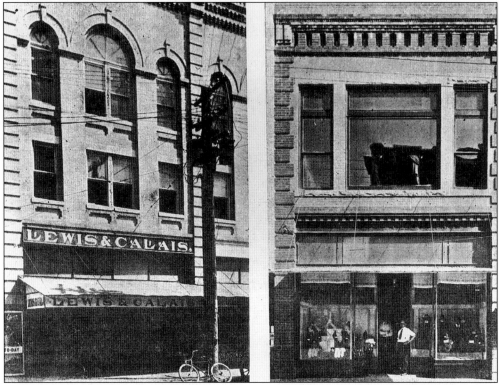

Lewis and Calais Ladies and Women's Outfitters, established *c.* 1911, was located at 144 West Main Street, next to the New Theatre, which was on the second floor of the Hodges Building. The New Theatre was operated by a stock company consisting of R.E. Hodges, Jay M. Hodges, J.L. Capehart, Sam Etheridge, and Tom Blow. (IN.)

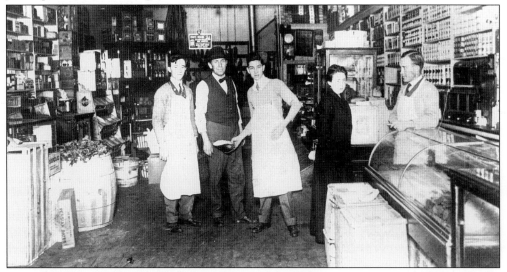

Walter Credle and Co., established *c.* 1913, was located at 157 West Main Street. Credle owned a three-story brick commercial structure built by J.S. Small and John Havens. This 1913 photo shows, from left to right, Pete Rhode, Walter Credle, and Charlie Wright (lady and clerk are unknown). (HR.)

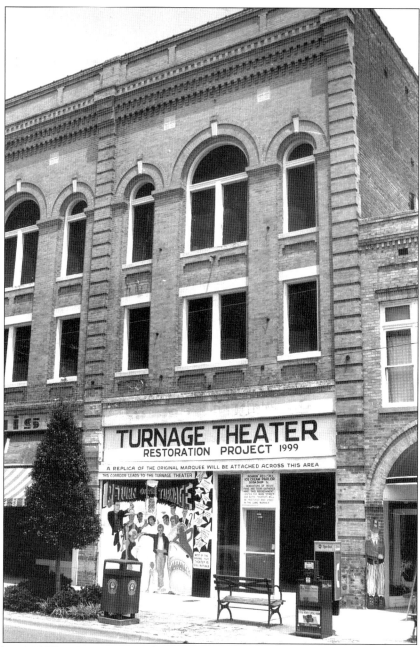

Located at 146 West Main Street, the Turnage Theatre remained in business from *c.* 1930 to 1976. C.A. Turnage leased this three-story building in 1929. As one entered, there was a small cafe, and N.E. Saleely had a fruit concession. Prior to 1928, Turnage had a street-level shoe store, which later became the promenade. The third floor housed the New Theatre of Vaudeville, which seated 400 people. Suburban families would ride the Atlantic Coast Line train to the Gladden Street depot and walk to the theater. When silent movies came, Turnage added a screen and modern film equipment; his first film was *Lord Byrum of Broadway*. Turnage also showed the first talking picture, *Lights of New York*. The next year, Turnage built a sound film theater on the ground floor, which seated 676. (VC.)

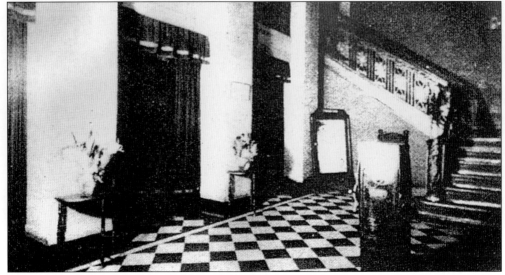

The lobby of the old Turnage Theatre "had the aura of a big city theater. It was most enchanting," recalled Judy Jennette, who saw movies there several times. A curved stairway led from the tiled lobby to the Turnage Theatre's balcony. The Turnage gave way to Washington's Cinema III, which opened in Washington Square Mall in 1976. (WT.)

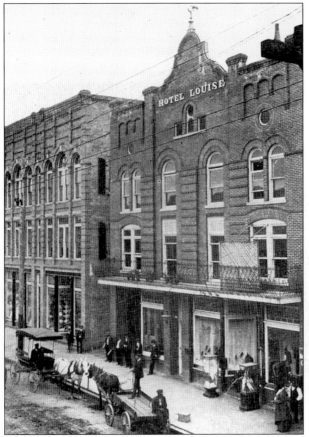

Shown here is the Hotel Louise, c. 1904, at 163–169 West Main Street. Owned by Thomas Archbell, this four-story brick commercial building had a handsome classical cornice, round arched openings, and many other fine details. Have you noticed the wooden sidewalks? The Louise had 75 rooms, 40 baths, and electric lights and was the only hotel in town with an elevator. It also had a third-floor dining room overlooking the Pamlico River. The Louise had several large horse-drawn buses with a porter at the rear. The porters were chosen for their personality, diplomacy, and line of chatter. The hotel buses would await passengers at the Atlantic Coast Line Railroad Depot on Gladden Street, and the porters would bow and solicit traveling salesmen, for they usually stayed for several days. The Louise closed in 1969 and was converted to the Hotel Louise Apartments. (PC OS.)

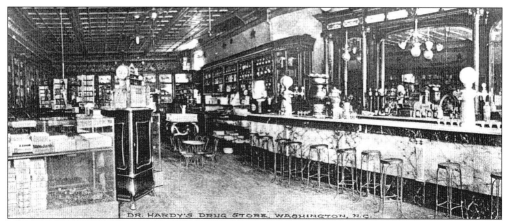

Located on the first floor of the Hotel Louise on Main Street, the Worthy & Etheridge Drug Store, established c. 1922, was Dr. Hardy's Drug Store in 1915. The Worthy had a fancy soda fountain and was a gathering place for locals and visitors alike. W & E carried a large selection of tobacco products and stick candies. (PC HR.)

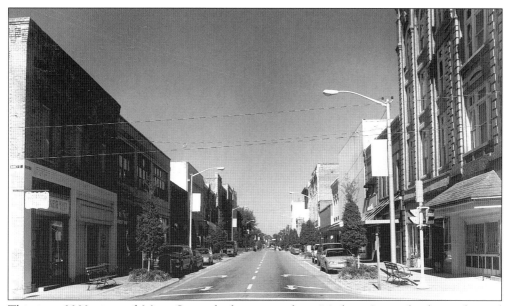

This is a 2000 view of Main Street looking west from Market. Car styles have changed considerably since 1937, and Main Street is now one way. In 1981 Washington's ongoing restoration project was rewarded when it was selected as a National Main Street Demonstration City, a city to serve as a model for others. (VC.)

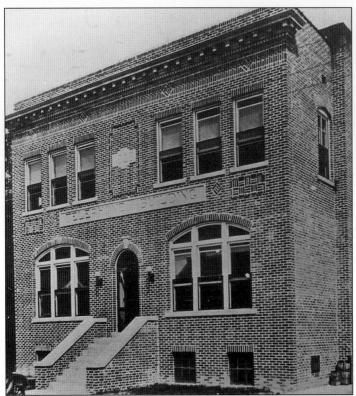

In 1896, the Washington Telephone Co. and the W.T. Thomas Telephone Co. ran a line from Bayboro to Aurora and up to Washington. The line ran down Main Street from Bridge to Market Streets. One would call "operator" and ask to speak to the desired party. In 1923, the Carolina Telephone and Telegraph Co. (CTT) took over and built a plain two-story brick structure at 123 Respass Street (now spelled Respess). This building was demolished and replaced by the Sprint Communications Center. (BRL.)

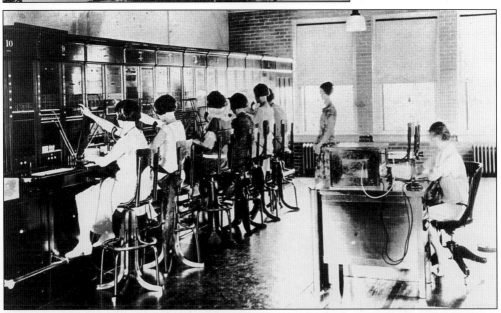

From 1923 until 1957, CTT operators handled the switchboard manually. Callers would say "central" and ask to be connected to a two- or three-digit number. Washington's first operator was Miss Josephine Whitney, whom everyone knew, and she, in turn, knew everyone's business. In 1957 CTT installed a dial system, and Washington was assigned the call letters "WH." (BRL.)

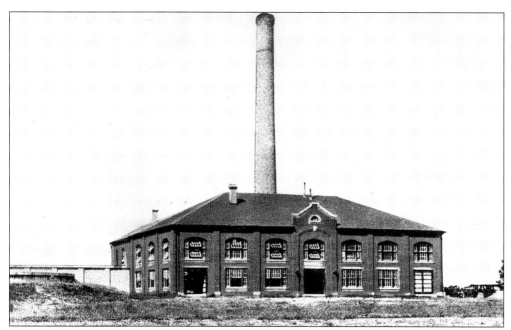

The second Washington Electric Co. operated from 1905 until 1913 and was located on the north side of Third Street, between Bridge and Van Norden Streets. It was equipped with two small dynamos and two steam engines. At first, current was furnished only for night lighting, but it later was supplied 24 hours a day. This plant served Washington, Aurora, Chocowinity, and Grimesland with electric power. (PC OS.)

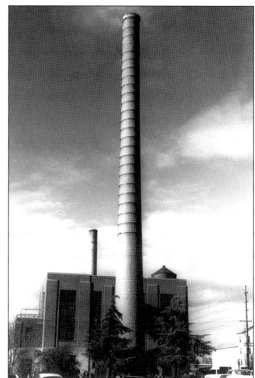

Washington's third power plant was erected in 1913 and was located at the intersection of Plymouth and West Third Streets. Its smokestack was 225 foot high. By the late 1940s, this plant was hard pressed to provide reliable electric service and was shut down in 1948 and then demolished in 1990. (Photo Benjy Allen; HR.)

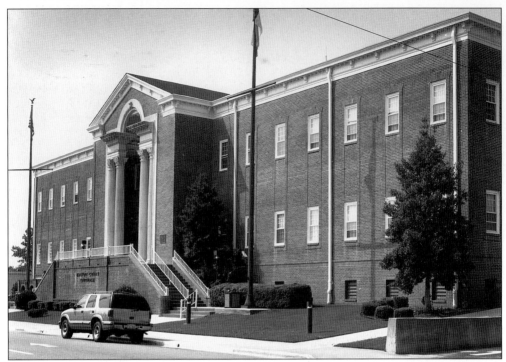

Located at 112 West Second Street, the Beaufort County Courthouse, constructed *c.* 1971, is a modern three-story brick building containing the offices of the Register of Deeds, civil court, county manager, district judges, adult probation parole, district attorney, grand jury, library, magistrates, jail, County Work Program, legal library, and Clerk of the Court. (VC.)

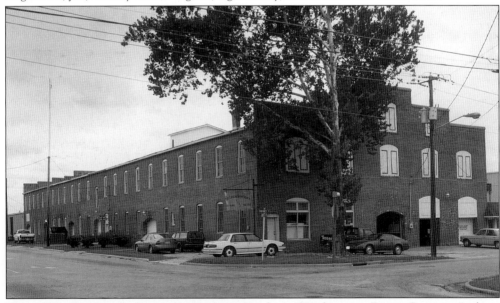

This 1999 photograph shows the Hackney Brothers "Washington Buggy Company" plant, located at the corner of Hackney and Third Streets. Railroad tracks ran on both sides of the plant building and into Eureka Lumber Co., situated on the Tar River's waterfront. This nicely renovated brick building is now occupied by East Carolina Import Services. (VC.)

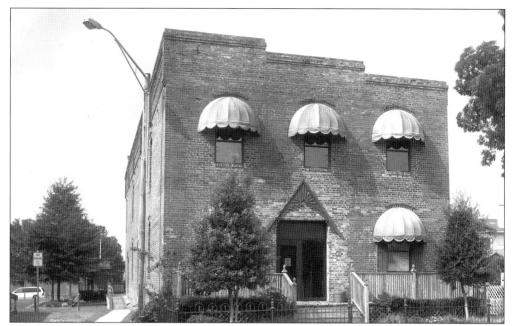

Started *c.* 1904, the E. Peterson Co. was located at 310 West Main Street, and its structure was built by J.F. Randolf, president and general manager of one of the largest wholesale grocery operations in Eastern North Carolina. Peterson used the railroad siding where the Atlantic Coast Line caboose is seen parked. Renovated in 1976 by builder Fred Mallison, the structure was developed into office space. The City of Washington purchased the site in 1994 and presently rents space to the Washington Senior Resources Center, the City of Washington Administrative Offices for Parks and Recreation, the Washington Civic Center, and the Partnership of the Sounds, Inc. (VC.)

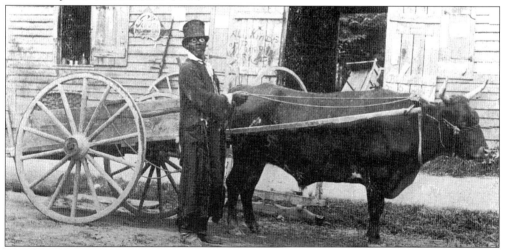

Dowdy "Waterproof" Mose and his "AutomoBULL" are pictured here, *c.* 1912. Mose, the son of Nathan Mose, was a drayman, and he paid the city $1 a year for an operator's license. For a drayman's service, people paid 10¢ a load or bundle, or 35¢ fare for a ride anywhere in town. Draymen were present for every train and boat arrival. Mose was also the proprietor of a grocery store and a butcher shop in the 100 block on Gladden Street, but he later moved his businesses to the corner of Harding and Respess Streets. (WL.)

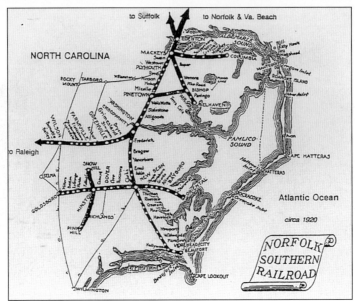

The first railroad in Beaufort County was the Jamesville to Washington route built in the 1870s. The line ran from the Roanoke River to Washington and down Washington Street to a depot and hotel. Shown above is the 1920 Norfolk Southern Railroad (NSR) track lines in North Carolina. The NSR still runs a freight train daily through Havens Gardens, to and from Chocowinity. Passenger trains gave way to the automobile as the state paved the roads in the 1920s and 1930s and development larger highways. The Norfolk Southern Railroad lines remain the same today as they were in 1920.

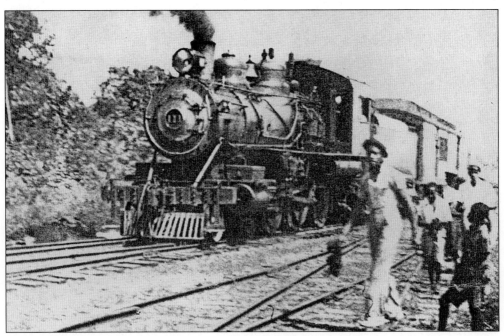

Here is the ten-wheeler engine No. 111, of the Norfolk Southern Railroad, backing onto the main line after unloading at the Washington terminal in 1937. (WS.)

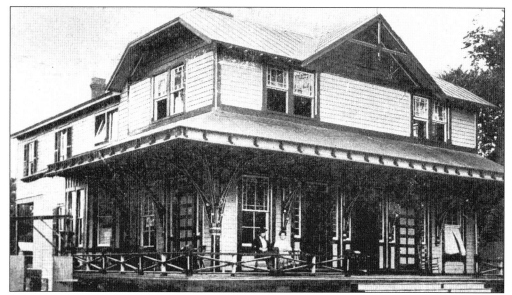

The Central Hotel, established c. 1912, was located on the corner of Third and Gladden Streets, near the Atlantic Coast Line (ACL) Depot. "New, neat and up-to date in all its appointments. Rates $1.00 to $1.50 per day," said proprietor J.R. Starling in 1912. (WL.)

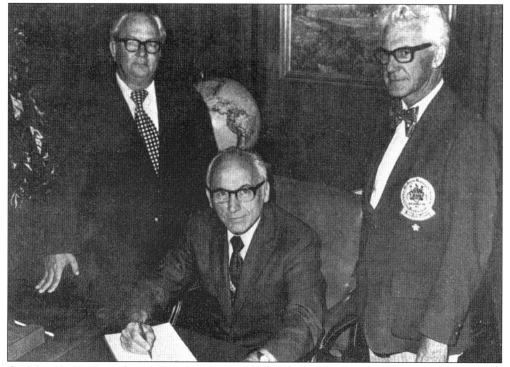

On May 20, 1975, Seaboard Coastline Railroad (SCR) gave the City of Washington possession of the old Gladden Street ACL station depot and warehouse. The city restored and remodeled the warehouse into a fine civic center. The depot was later converted into office space. From left to right are Mayor Max Roebuck, J.C. Clark, and Roland Modlin (vice president of SCR and Bicentennial Commission chairman), who is signing the document. (WDN.)

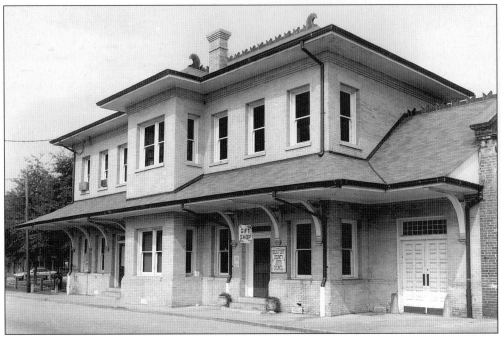

The ACL Depot on Gladden Street was built for $12,000 in 1904. S.R. Clary was the ticket agent in 1918. ACL ran until 1975, when the city acquired the depot. The second floor was cleaned of soot, and the space was rented to the Beaufort County Arts Council in September 1975. When first-floor renovations were completed, the Arts Council moved downstairs, and in 1985 the upstairs was rented to the Pamlico Tar River Foundation. (VC.)

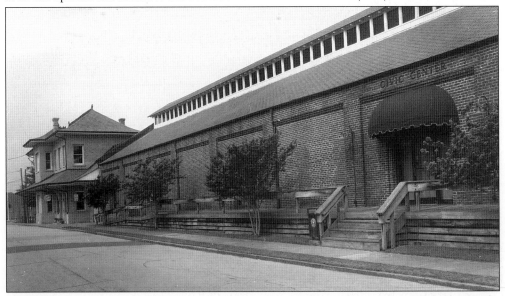

The Washington Civic Center, located at 116 North Gladden Street, was formerly the freight annex of the Atlantic Coast Line. It has a series of large arched openings and handsome doors. The center is used for art shows, entertainment, conventions, and weddings. The Crape Myrtles that adorn either side of the center were authorized by Mayor R.P. MacKenzie, and Charles Smallwood planted most of these lovely trees. (VC.)

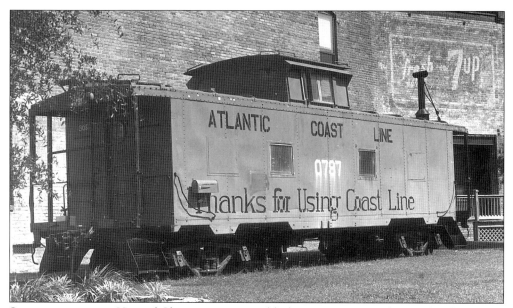

State representative Howard Chapin was responsible for getting ACL to donate the old caboose parked behind the train depot on Gladden Street. In 1892, the City of Washington paid the Atlantic Coast Line $10,000 to run tracks here. ACL completed the job in 1904, and passenger and freight business boomed until the mid-1930s. In 1905, ACL had a daily round-trip run to Parmele, where trains from Kinston, Greenville, Rocky Mount, Plymouth, Weldon, and Tarboro met and exchanged passengers and mail. Captain Ellsworth was the conductor and Ed Leens was engineer. (VC.)

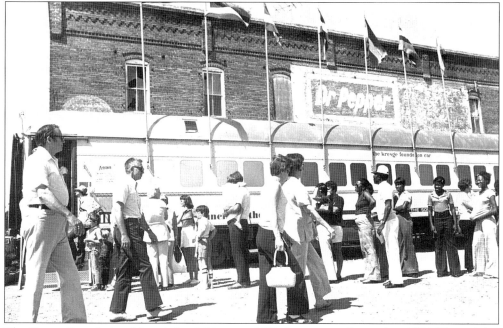

The Kresge Foundation "Artrain" exhibit visited Washington in September 1974. The exhibit was displayed in a Kresge Pullman passenger train parked behind the train depot where the ACL caboose was parked in the early 1990s. (BRL.)

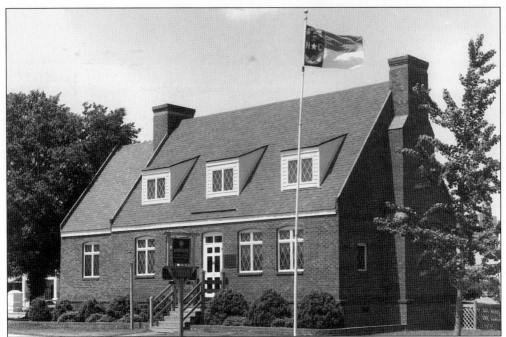

Located on Stewart Parkway, the Washington Beaufort County Chamber of Commerce office building is a replica of the Newbold White house in Hertford. Visitors and interested parties can obtain brochures and information at the chamber of commerce for the Historic Washington Walking Tour and the Tour of Historic Churches of Washington, North Carolina—both self-guided tours. (VC.)

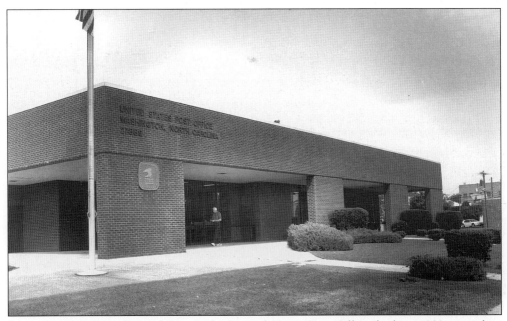

Located at 222 West Second Street, the United States Post Office, built *c.* 1980, is a plain modern one-story brick building. Handling an average of 300,000 pieces of mail a week, the post office delivers to 20,000 city and rural families on weekdays and on Saturday. (VC.)

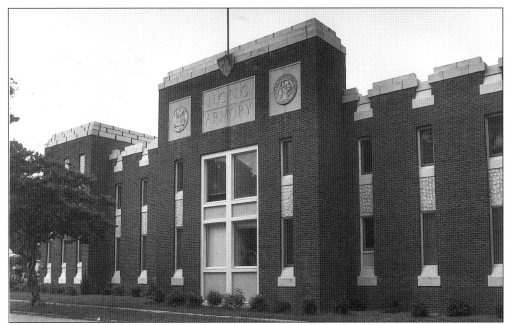

The North Carolina Armory, built c. 1935, was Washington's second armory—the first having been located in the old "Market" building at the foot of Market Street, which burned down in 1900. Located on Jack's Creek at the end of East Main Street, the armory served as the training center for Battery "C" of the 113th Field Artillery Battalion of the 30th N.C. National Guard Division. It was also used as a civic center for dances and Beaufort County basketball tournaments. The 30th Division was mobilized when President Roosevelt declared an "Unlimited National Emergency" in September 1940. A new armory building was constructed in 1976 at the end of Minuteman Lane, and armory was sold and converted into apartments. (VC.)

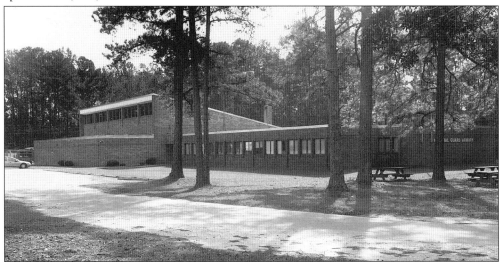

Located at 399 Minuteman Lane, the North Carolina Army National Guard (NCANG), c. 1976, was Washington's third armory building. It is used by the 213th Military Police Co. and was Headquarter 167 for the military police battalion until October 1996. In 2000 it is occupied by the NCANG Detachment 1 HHC, 1/119th Mechanical Infantry. (VC.)

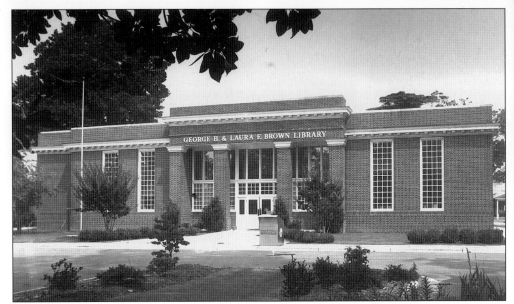

Located at 122 Van Norden Street, the George H. and Laura E. Brown Library, c. 1954, began in the Brown home in 1944, and this building was completed in 1954. This private library was funded by interest earned from investments of the Brown estate until 1989, when the City of Washington took ownership. The Friends of the Brown Library, a non-profit group, raise additional money every year to help enhance the library program. (VC.)

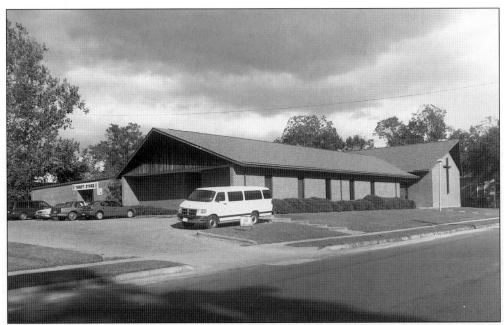

The Salvation Army Building, c. 1934, is located at 112 East Seventh Street. Envoy Charles Cook, who came from New Bern, opened a post in Washington in 1934. In 1937 Captain Iona Pope established the Corps as a self-supporting unit. The Corps has grown dramatically in recent years and did a magnificent job under the direction of Major Samuel J. Bivens, helping those who had lost everything in Hurricane Floyd in 1999. (VC.)

Four
CHURCHES, SCHOOLS, HOSPITALS, AND PUBLIC BUILDINGS
1900–1999

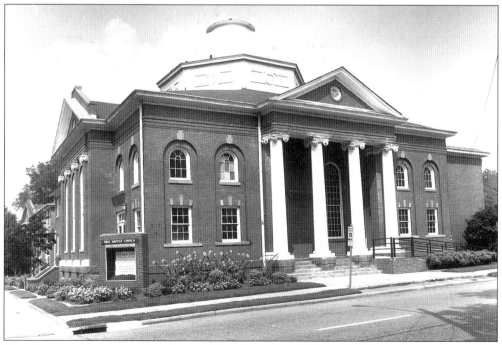

This photograph shows the First Baptist Church, built c. 1916, at 113 North Harvey Street. The original church was built in 1822 on Market Street, across from the post office. By 1896 the congregation was so large it was necessary to renovate and enlarge the church, and in 1916 the members decided to build a new church. An educational building was added in 1956. (VC.)

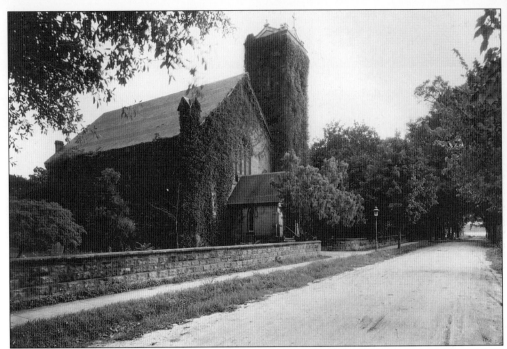

Located on the corner of Bonner and East Main Streets, St. Peter's Episcopal Church, *c.* 1867, is a classic Gothic-style church with lovely stained-glass windows. The pews were installed in 1885, and the wood ceiling, the slate roof, and the tower were added in 1893. The parish house was completed in 1959. (1910 PH, courtesy WM.)

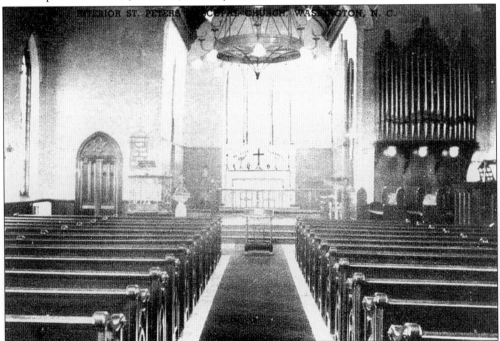

This interior of St. Peter's Episcopal Church was photographed around 1915. The picture has been redrawn, and the airbrush retouching causes the whitish look. (WM.)

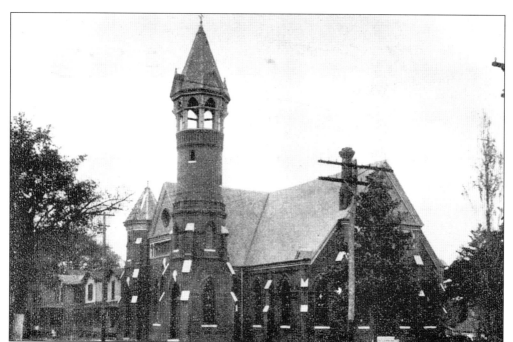

The First United Methodist Church, c. 1898, is seen here at 304 West Second Street. The Methodist Society was formed in 1784. In 1831, Mrs. Sarah Katherine Quinn donated the Second Street land site, and a church, which was later burned down during the Civil War, was built at that location. The present church was erected in 1899 by architect Charles Hartge. (1915 PC OS.)

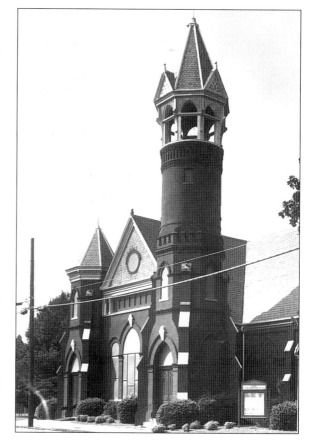

This splendid Victorian Gothic brick church is a Charles Hartge architectural treasure. Notice the cross gable slate roof, corner tower, and many quality ornamental details. The Educational Building—now the Administration Building—was added in 1918, the chapel was constructed in 1952, and the annex was built in 1970. (VC.)

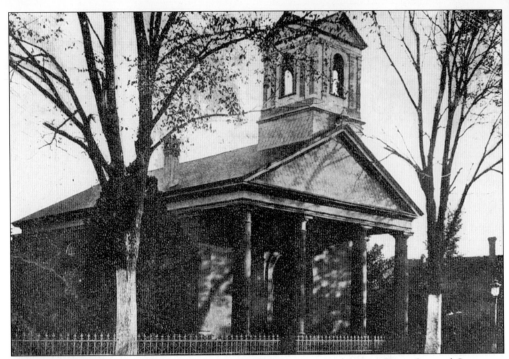

Located at 211 West Second Street, the First Presbyterian Church's original church structure was built in 1823, burned during the Civil War, and, rebuilt in 1867. During the war, the congregation donated its bell to be melted down for bullets. After the war, Presbyterian women collected 1000 pounds of scrap metal and shipped it north to be cast into a new bell. On the return trip, the cargo ship *Catherine Johnson* was wrecked off Cape Hatteras. All cargo was lost except the bell, which washed ashore, was salvaged, returned, and now rings daily. (PC OS.)

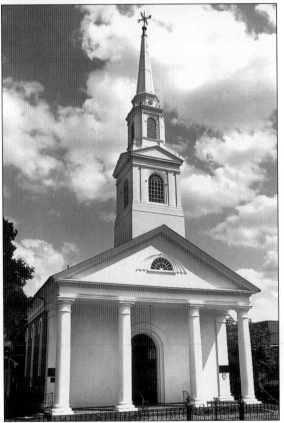

The entrance to First Presbyterian Church is located on Gladden Street. Interior alterations were made to the church in 1890. The high pulpit was lowered, circular stairs were installed, and the fluted columns were removed. In 1952, a steeple was erected and the interior of the sanctuary was renovated. (VC.)

The Metropolitan African Methodist Episcopal Zion Church is located at 100 West Fourth Street. Founded in 1841, the present church was built in 1909. This brick Romanesque-style church has crenelated towers, granite lintels, sills, and keystones. The exterior finish is pressed brick with colored glass windows. The Metropolitan AME Zion Church has over 300 parishioners and is the largest black church in North Carolina. From 1865 until about 1915, the church operated a school for blacks in the lower levels of it building. The church has a wonderful 1891 George Jardine pipe organ, which has 350 wooden and metal pipes. (VC.)

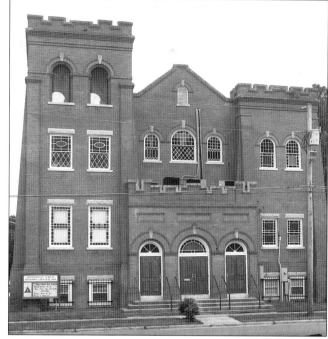

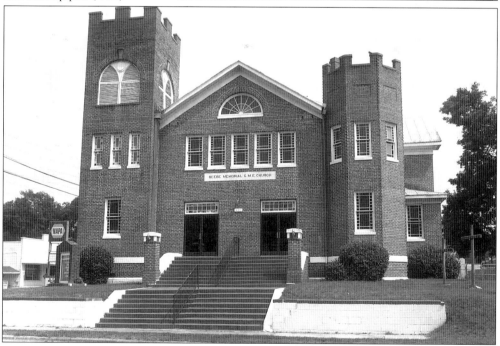

Located at 131 West Fifth Street, the Beebe Memorial (formerly the Christian Temple) Colored Methodist Episcopal Church, c. 1927, is a Gothic Revival-style brick church. In 1871 Reverend J.A. Beebe came from his parish in Edenton and organized the Christian Temple CME, which was built in 1873. This was the first black Methodist Episcopal church erected in North Carolina. The Beebe Chapel on U.S. 17, near Cherry Run Road, was named in his honor. (VC.)

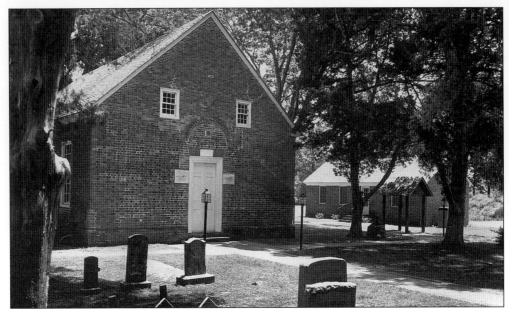

St. Thomas Episcopal Church in Bath, *c.* 1734, is the oldest existing church in North Carolina. This church was built of English-made brick and laid in the Flemish-bond pattern; the floor was made of English tile. (VC.)

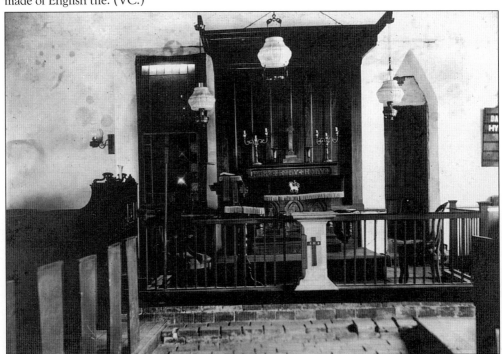

The interior of St. Thomas Church has two rows of pews with aisles leading down each side and the middle. This 1915 picture by T.R. Draper shows that the church had gas lamps. However, there are several valuable relics not shown: a three-branched candelabra from King George II (*c.* 1740); the Queen Anne's bell, cast in England in 1732; a large English Bible from 1703; and a 1733 hand-wrought silver chalice from the bishop of London. (TD, courtesy WM.)

Our Mother of Mercy Catholic Church, built c. 1929, is located at 112–114 West Ninth Street. The first Catholic church in Washington, St. John the Evangelist, was formed in 1824 and was located on the corner of Third and Van Norden Streets. It burned in 1864 during the Civil War. The Mother of Mercy parish, a mission church and a school for blacks, was formed in 1925. In 1929, St. Agnes Chapel (seen here) was built, and St. Agnes Academy, a parochial school for whites, opened in 1939. In 1963, the two Catholic parishes and their schools integrated and became one parish and one school. Lack of funding closed the school in 1973. (VC.)

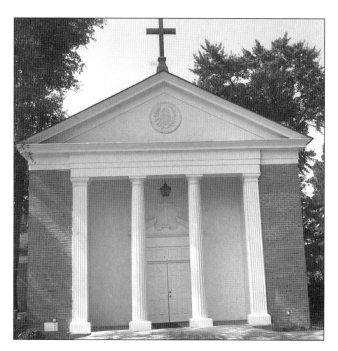

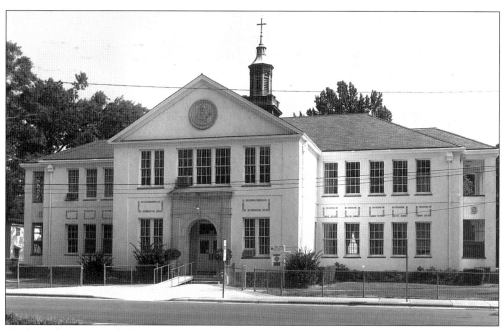

Mother of Mercy Catholic School was the first integrated school in Washington. After a long struggle with declining enrollment, Mother of Mercy School closed on May 30, 1973. The school is now used as offices and a community hall. (VC.)

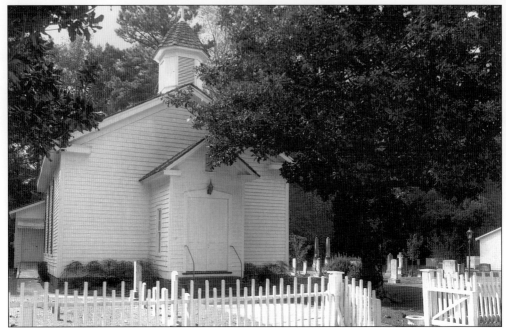

This is Zion Episcopal Church, built *c.* 1856, and its rectory, constructed in 1884. The church, located on U.S. 264, was founded by Robert and Lucy Cutler in 1738. This poem, titled "The Church in the Wildwood," describes the charm and grace of the church: "Oh, come to the church in the wildwood, / To the trees where the wild flowers bloom; / Where the parting hymn will be chanted, / We will weep by the side of the tomb. / How sweet on a clear Sabbath morning, / To list to the clear ringing bell; / Its tones so sweetly are calling, / Oh come to the church in the vale." (VC.)

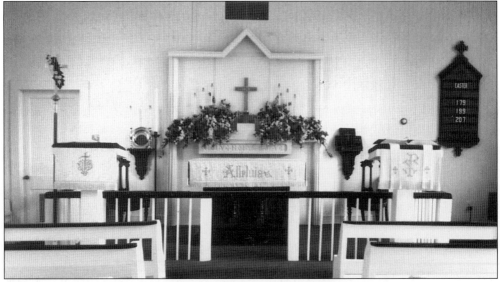

The altar of Zion Episcopal Church is seen here as it appeared in 2000. The church possesses a fine pipe organ, which has 13 stops and 18 ranks of pipes. In 1996, organist Douglas E. Cutler purchased this fine W. Zimmer & Sons of Charlotte, North Carolina organ for the church from East Carolina University's Fletcher Recital Hall. (HY.)

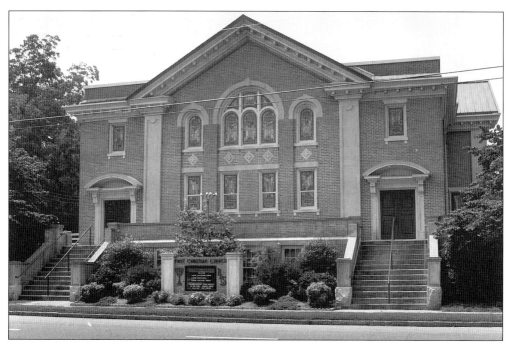

In 1926, popular church architect McMichael, of Charlotte, designed the First Christian Church, located at 401 East Second Street. A fine robust Neoclassic design, this church is built of buff brick and has a cruciform plan on a high basement with a wide terrace reached by double stairs. An educational building was dedicated in 1963. (VC.)

Asbury United Methodist Church was built *c.* 1856 on land donated by Thomas D. Smaw Sr. at 88 North Asbury Church Road off U.S. 264. In 1897, the very high pulpit was removed. In 1928, a bell was acquired from a discontinued Pinetown Methodist Church. In 1930 the vestibule and belfry tower were erected, and the bell was hung. The Sunday school annex was added in 1940. (VC.)

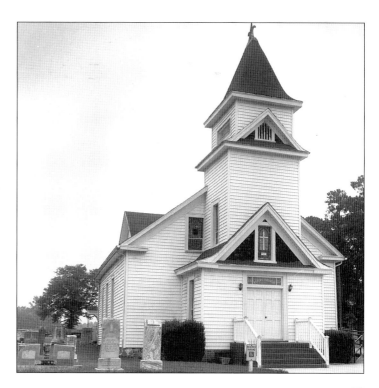

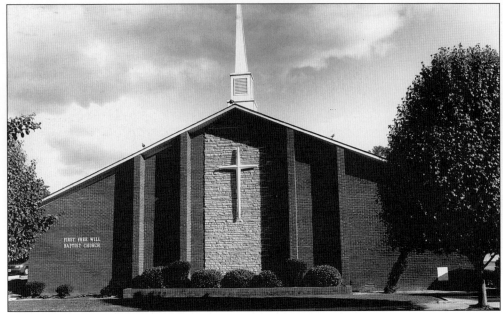

The First Free Will Baptist Church, built c. 1951, is located at 901 North Bonner Street. The original church was built before 1800 on lot No. 50 and was used by all denominations. In 1958 a new parsonage was built on the adjoining lot. An educational building was completed in 1961. The church was bricked, carpeted, and the steeple was added in 1970. In 1955 the church started a Sunday School Mission on River Road, which became Mizpah Free Will Baptist Church. (VC.)

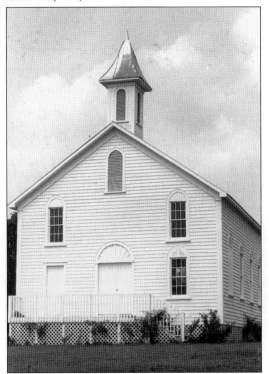

The Singleton Primitive Baptist Church, built by its members c. 1891, was founded by John R. Rowe, Tevu and George Roberson, Henry Peel, J.J. Smith, and D.W.Topping. The church was named after the widow of John C. Singleton, who donated the land. The original land site was across the street from the Fire Station on Market and Fifth Streets. Singleton was restored in 1996–97 by the Washington Area Historic Foundation and moved to Creekside Road, off U.S. 264 West. (VC.)

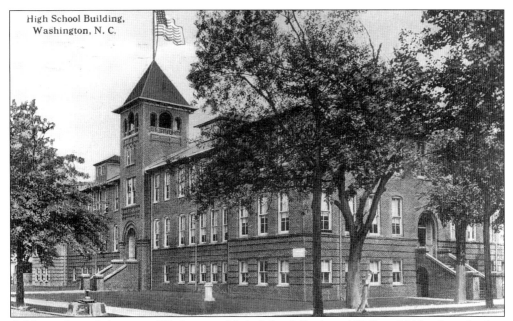

High School Building, Washington, N. C.

Athletics for girls began at Washington High School (built *c.* 1906) in 1915, when the first basketball team was organized by Miss Lura Brogden (Mrs. Herbert Gravely). The players were Sally Bright (Mrs. Albert Edwards), Dorothy Blount (Mrs. Hugh Anderson), Elizabeth McIlhenny (Mrs. Zack Koonce), Leonora Blount (Mrs. James Kelly), and Mildred Smith (Mrs. John Johnson). (PC OS.)

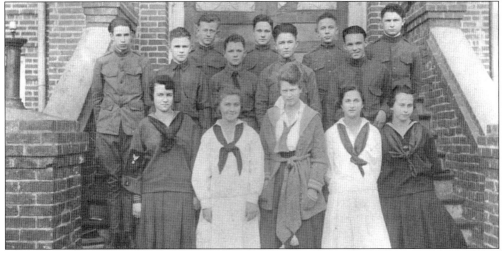

This is the Washington High School Senior Class of 1919. They are, from left to right, as follows: (front row) Athalia Cotten Tayloe, Bertha Rosenthal Susman, Elizabeth Carmen Tibbatts, Myra Louise Arthur, and Annie Thomas Archbell; (second row) Sylvester Fleming Hodges, Benjamin Louis Susman Jr., Guy Hodges Cooper, William Whiting McIlhenny, and Frank Kugler Baker; (third row) John William Oden, Jack Warren, Dan Lee Simmons, and Robert Thomas Johnson. Not shown are Mary Sheppard Parker and Reva Mae Jefferson. William McIlhenny's brother, Harry H. McIlhenny, graduated from the Annapolis Class of 1927 and rose to the rank of rear admiral. The class motto was "Not finished—just begun." (CCX.)

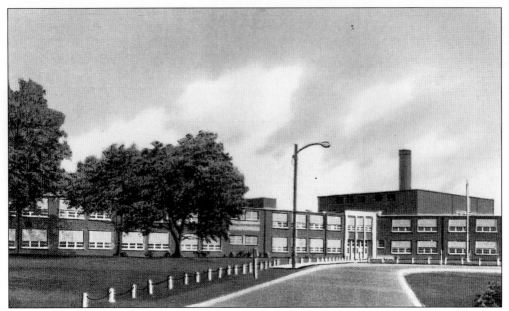

Washington's second high school was located at 820 Bridge Street and opened in 1950. When Washington's third high school (pictured below) opened in 1951, this school was renamed the P.S. Jones Middle School after Peter Simon Jones, a fine black teacher who moved to Washington in 1927 to teach black youths.

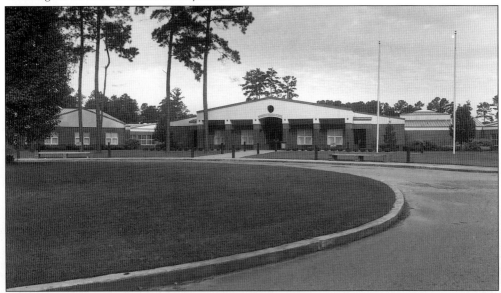

This photograph captures Washington High School (WHS), built c. 1991 and located at 400 Slatestone Road. The school's 1998 enrollment was 1,039. It contains grades nine through twelve and has its own internet site. Known for its fine educational tradition, the faculty at WHS select 20 students each year for the Who's Who list of students who best represent the idea of achievement. WHS has a wide array of activities for students, including 27 sports programs, the *Packromak Yearbook* (under the guidance of teacher Cathy Cox), *Opus* magazine, and *Currents*, the school newspaper (both magazine and newspaper under the direction of teacher Susan Wellborn). (VC.)

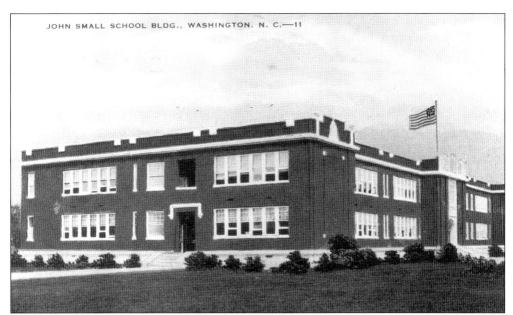

The John C. Small School began *c.* 1923 and closed in 1990, being demolished in 1998. This handsome brick grade school shows a notable Gothic-style that includes blind tracery in the entrance pavilion, Tudor arches, rosettes, and simple crenellations. The name John Small School was transferred to the former P.S. Jones School at 820 Bridge Street. (PC OS.)

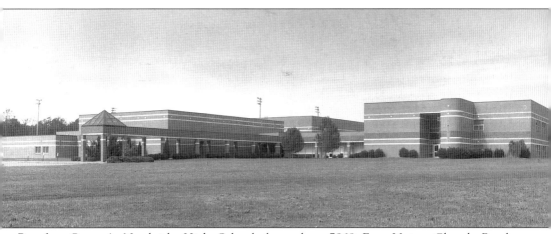

Beaufort County's Northside High School, located at 7868 Free Union Church Road, serves grades 9 through 12 for the people of eastern Beaufort County and a section of Washington County. With a 1999 enrollment of 556 students, the school offers seven sports programs. (VC.)

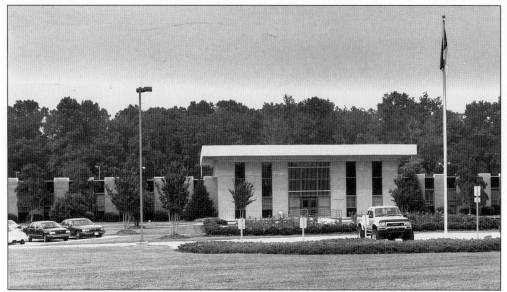

Beaufort County Community College (BCCC) is located on U.S. 264 some 4 miles east of U.S. 17. An accredited two-year technical college, BCCC was founded in 1971 as a consolidation of the Beaufort County Technical Institute. The college offers both day and evening accredited courses and many other non-credit courses. (VC.)

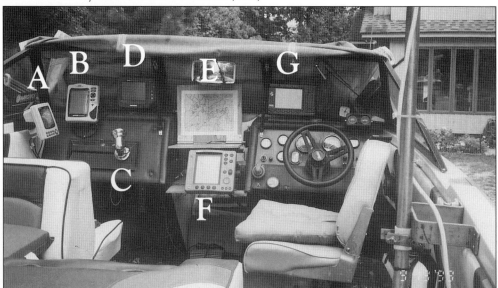

This is a typical small boat cockpit display: (A & D) Sonar; (B) Global Positioning System (GPS); (C) VHF Radio; (E) computer NOS Charting; (F) radar; and (G) DGPS. BCCC offers a course in small boat navigation systems by instructor Stanton Prentiss, who says, "Today's small boat navigation systems are all electronic, compact, reliable, and accurate to within a few feet. The instrumentation is anchored by a 24 satellite GPS and aided by some 50 Coast Guard Differential DGPS Beacon precision land-correction installations. These can also be assisted by sonar, radar, and VHF radio, plus the Federal Aviation Wide Area Augmentation System (WAAS) for aircraft, land, and sea guidance. In addition, vector (plug-in) and NOS (Federal charts) can offer printout land mapping and sea charting upon command. (SP.)

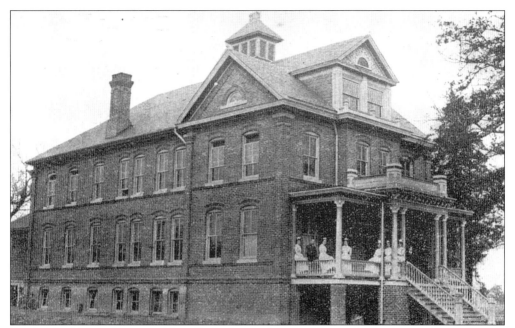

Funded by Robert Bruce, a New York doctor friend of James L. Fowle, in the amount of $12,500, Fowle Memorial Hospital was incorporated in 1902 by James L. Fowle and Doctors William A. Blount, Samuel T. Nicholson, David T. Tayloe, and Edwin M. Brown for the dual purpose of treatment and education. The hospital, built c. 1904, was located at the corner of Market and Fifth Streets and was later demolished. (PC OS.)

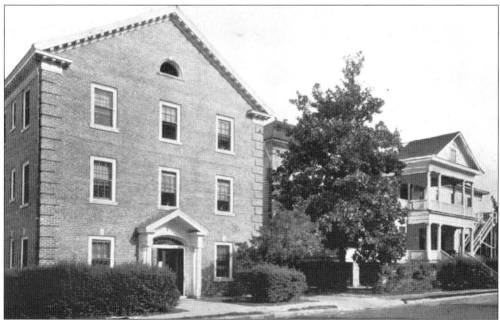

Built c. 1908 on Washington Street, Tayloe Hospital, now closed, was a three-story Colonial-style brick building (visible on the left), and the hospital was founded by Doctors David and Joshua Tayloe. The frame building on the right was the original hospital, which burned down around 1940. (PC BL.)

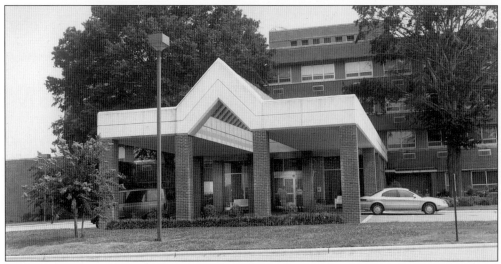

Dr. John Cotten Tayloe was the first chief of staff for the Beaufort County Hospital, located at the corner of Highland and Hudnell Streets. BCH was built in 1958 as a 142-bed, not-for-profit, public hospital, and it offers a wide range of health services to citizens of Beaufort, Pamlico, Martin, and Washington Counties. The medical staff consists of some 42 physicians (practicing 20 different specialties) and prides itself on serving the area with progressive health care. (VC.)

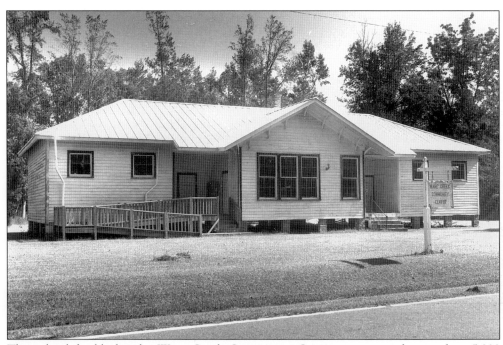

This school for blacks, the Ware Creek Community Center, was one of more than 5,000 Rosenwald schools built between 1917 and 1932. Dr. Booker T. Washington inspired philanthropist Julius Rosenwald to direct this 1930s WPA project in Ware Creek. (VC.)

80

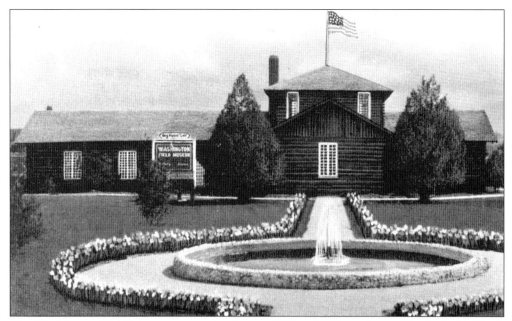

The Washington Field Museum, operating from c. 1923 to 1945, was located in the Jack's Creek area. This teaching museum was lovingly referred to by locals as the "Bug House." In the summer of 1923, four 13-year-old boys—George Ross, John Radcliff, James Braddy, and Dick Dunston—started a bug and plant collection in a burlap tent, and by 1926, their bug collection was so large that it had to be moved to a wooden shack on East Fifth Street. In 1934, with WPA assistance, a log building and fountain garden was completed in the City Park at the end of Second and Charlotte Streets. It was North Carolina's first all "artificial light" museum. (PC OS.)

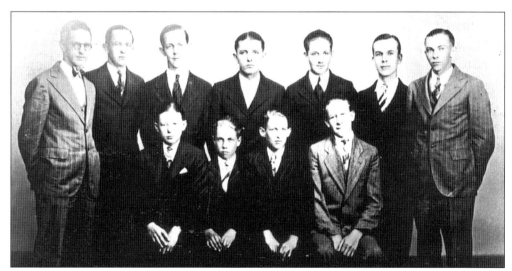

"Bug House" members pose for a portrait at Baker's Studio in March 1928. They are, from left to right, as follows: (seated) Blake Lewis, William Blount "Gimlet" Laughinghouse, Churchill Bragaw, and David Ross; (standing) Richard Dunston, George Ross, Harold Yert, James Braddy, Owen Mclean, Zoph Potts, and Donnie Morris. The club motto was "What the Bug House can't do, can't be done." (ES.)

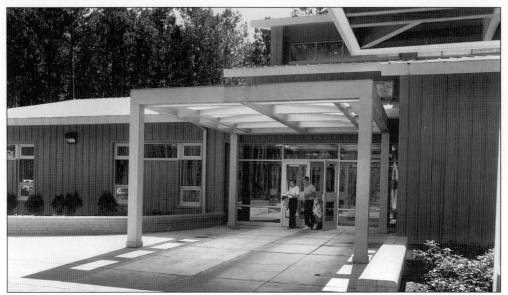

Visitors Mary E. (Lib) Daniels and Mary Alice Chapin are pictured here exiting the Goose Creek State Park Environmental Education/Visitors Center. This fine park borders on Goose Creek and the Pamlico River 8 miles east of Washington off U.S. 264. The park features several walking trails and offers dry camping and canoeing, numerous family nature programs, and free classroom time to non-profit groups. (VC.)

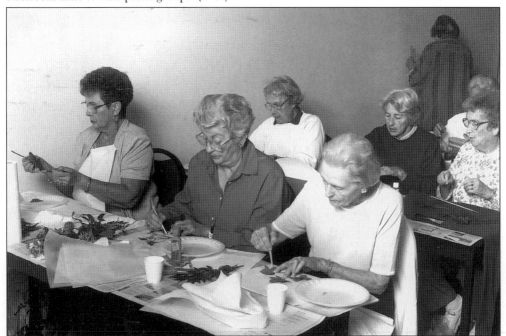

During a 1999 autumn workshop, Shirley Comish instructed a lab room filled with Washington Garden Club members in the art of "leaf stenciling" at the visitors center at Goose Creek State Park. They are, from left to right, as follows: (front row) Jayne Bennett, Mary Alice Chapin, and Mary (Lib) Daniels; (second row) Martha Kuehn, Priscilla Davidson, and Iveline (Ike) Czuhai. (VC.)

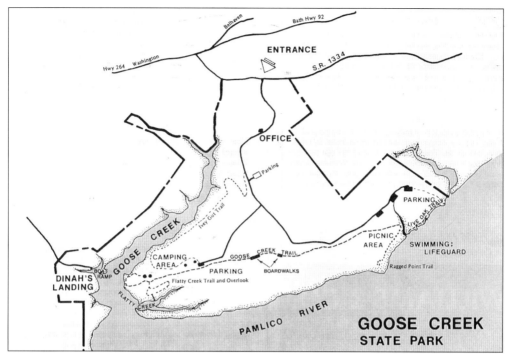

This is a map of Goose Creek Park.

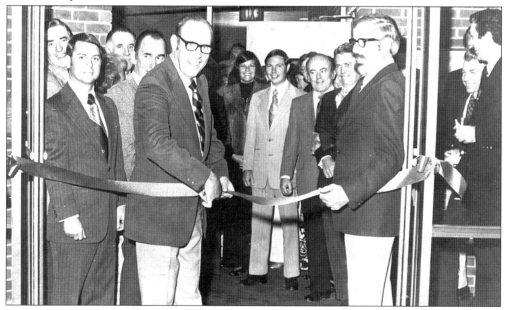

On December 29, 1973, the Washington Yacht & Country Club opened its new building at the end of River Road with a ribbon cutting. There were 183 members, with wives and guests in attendance. The Selby Jones orchestra played, and club manager Charlie Gast prepared a delicious meal. The people seen here are, from left to right, as follows: (left side, front) Hodges Hackney and (left side, rear) Hoss Thompson; (second row) Bob McDonough, Tom Stewart, and Clark Rodman, holding the ribbon; (third row center) Connie Hackney, Jim Hackney, Jim Williams, Tom Rivers, and Harold Lane; (right side, rear) Ace Mann and Fred Howdy. (WY.)

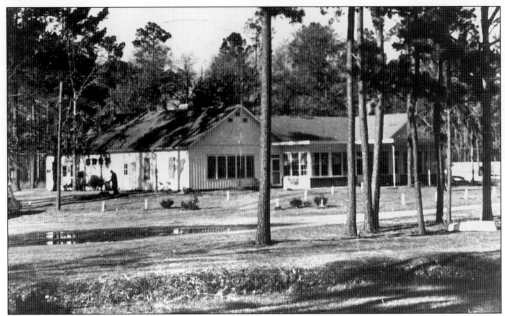

The Washington Yacht and Country Club's (WY&CC) clubhouse was being renovated when, on the night of November 21, 1971, it burned down. Club president Harold Lane appointed Clark Rodman as chairman of the building committee, and plans were made to build a new clubhouse. (WY.)

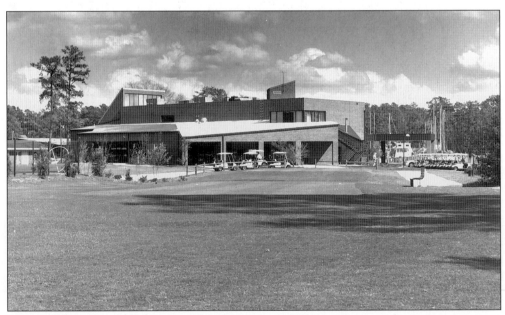

The new WY&CC clubhouse opened on December 7, 1973. It is larger and more contemporary in design than the old one. Nine new holes were added, making it an official USGA 18-hole course. During the 1996–98 seasons, a sprinkler system was installed, a lunchroom and bar called the 19th Hole was added, and the dining room was expanded. (VC.)

Five

THE HISTORIC HOMES DISTRICT

FROM 1760

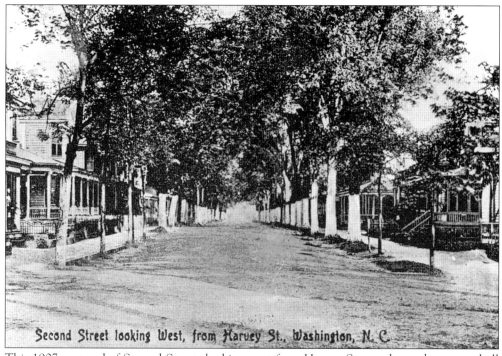

This 1907 postcard of Second Street, looking west from Harvey Street, shows the oyster shell street and sidewalks used at that time. The homes on the left side are the E.K. Willis House and the George Diamond House. E.K. Willis ran a ships store, and George Diamond and his brother Pete ran the Diamond Cafe on Main Street. On the right side of the postcard are the Robert Mitchell House, the Willy Bell House, and the W.H. Baker House. Mitchell ran a bar, Bell had a jewelry store, and Baker was the town's commercial and portrait photographer. (PC OS.)

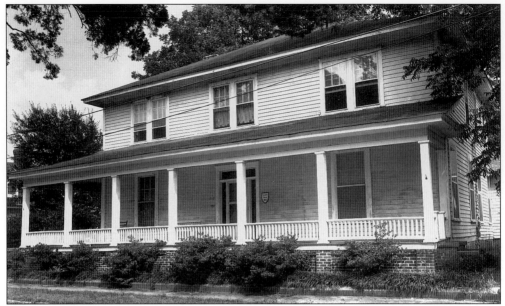

The Tannahill House was constructed *c.* 1842 at 113 Harvey Street. Tannahill & Lavender built the first sawmill in Washington in 1831. Tannahill had another partnership: Tannahill & Saunders, which owned the steamship *Edmund D. McNair*, a side-wheeler built by the Myers shipyard in 1835. They ran the *McNair* on the Tar River for many years. During the Civil War, the Tannahill House was used as a hospital from 1863 to 1864 by Union troops. From the late 1800s until 1906, Tannahill House served as the Episcopal rectory. In 2000, Tannahill House, owned by Steven Radar, was being used as a three-family apartment house. (VC.)

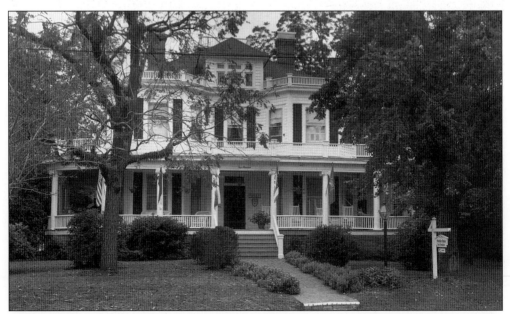

The original St. Peters Church Rectory, built *c.* 1906, is located at 400 East Main Street. This home was built to house the Reverend Nathaniel Harding and his family. It is now called the Pamlico House Bed & Breakfast and is owned by George and Jane Fields. (VC.)

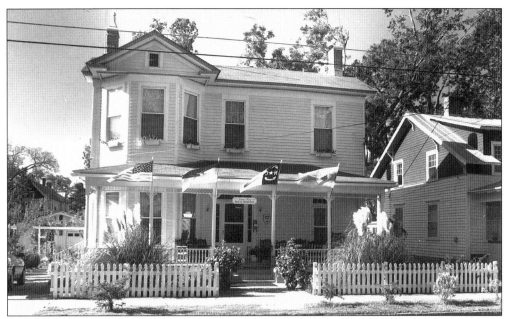

This photograph shows the the Tom Carawan House, built *c.* 1880 and located at 227 East Second Street. Carawan worked as a carpenter. The house is now called the Carolina House Bed & Breakfast and is run by Toni and Peter Oser, who renovated this fine old home in 1997. (VC.)

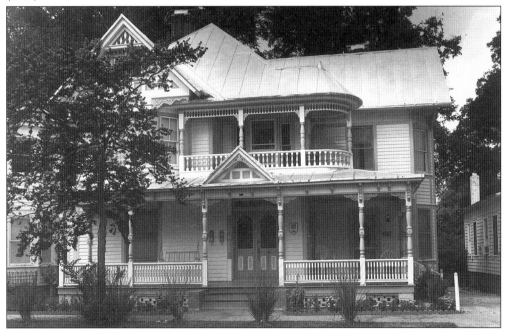

An exceptional Queen Anne-style house with Eastlake-style porch posts, the Minor House, built *c.* 1890, is located at 232 East Second Street. It has multiple gables, bay windows, sawn and turned detail, and an irregular shape. Sarah Minor was a grade school teacher in the McNair building school from 1903 until 1905, when it burned. Today, the home is owned by Peter and Toni Oser. (VC.)

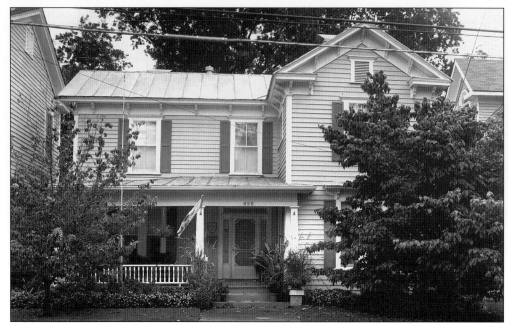

Located at 622 West Second Street, the Gilbert Rumley House, built *c.* 1893, is a two-story frame residence with simple details. The Rumleys had 13 children, of which only 5 survived to adulthood. Their daughter Mildred became Mildred Rumley Mayo. Gilbert Rumley was the register of deeds in 1913, and his son William was the sheriff in the early 1940s. John and Barbara Smith have restored the house to its original splendor. (VC.)

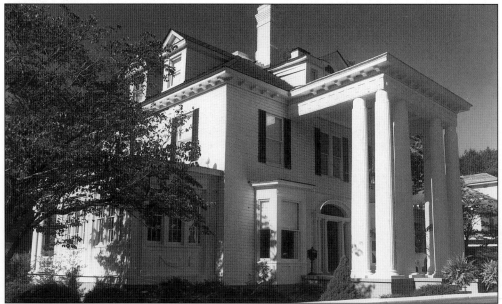

The Stephen C. Bragaw House, built *c.* 1898 at 127 East Second Street, is a handsome two-and-a-half-story Neo-Classical-style house, which belonged to Superior Court Judge Stephen C. Bragaw. Bragaw was born in Washington in 1868 and died 1930. He resigned from the First Judicial Court in 1914 because of poor health and joined the law firm of Harding, Ward, Small, MacLean and Bragaw. The present-day owners are Donald and Amanda Stroud. (VC.)

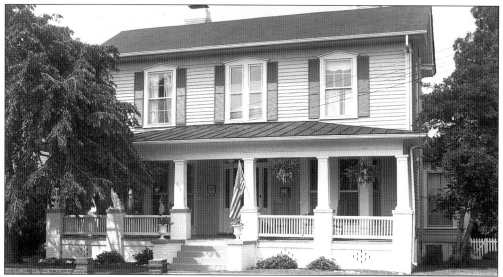

Built c. 1885 at 328 West Main Street, the N.S. Fulford House is a large two-story frame home with a 1920s-style porch, pediment window trim, and molded detail. The Fulford Hardware Store was a wholesale distributor located at 112 East Main Street from 1885 until 1907. The present-day owners are Archie and Lydie Jennings. (VC.)

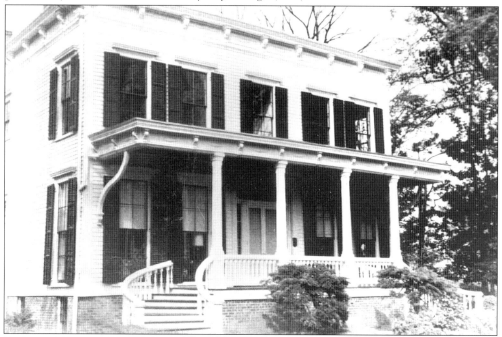

Built c. 1857 at 706 West Second Street, the Hollyday House is an Italianate structure that features period trim, including notable porch ornamentation, molded doors, window shutters, and a brick foundation. Built by George Brown, founder of the Bank of Washington, the Hollyday House served as a hospital during the Civil War. Holly Russ, who lived in the house during the 1920s, was a liberated woman, for she played golf and went fishing and hunting with her men friends. Mr. and Mrs. Mitchell Norton restored the house to its original stately grace in 1979. (OP.)

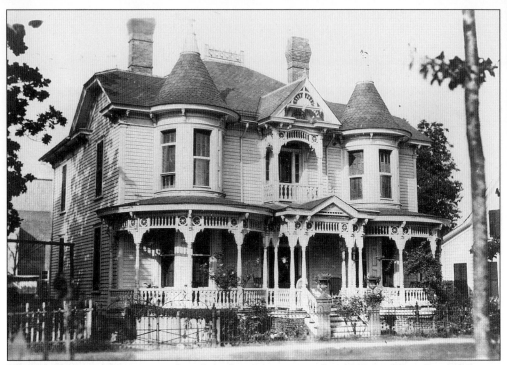

The J.F. Buckman Home, now demolished, was constructed *c.* 1898 on West Second Street. This Georgian-style double turret house had some interesting ship's wheel ornamentation around the porch. Buckman was one of the organizers of the "Washington at Christmas" parade back in 1885. (BK.)

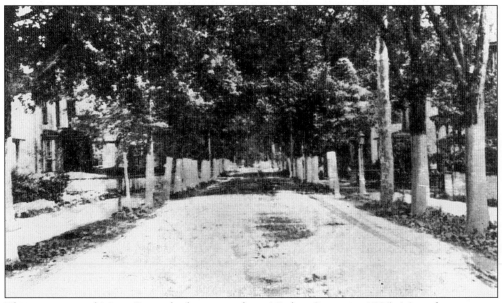

This is a view of Main Street looking east from Market Street in 1895. Many homes were demolished to make room for business expansion between 1900 and 1915, including the Patrician Inn and the Dimock home, where Susan Dimock was born. (PC OS.)

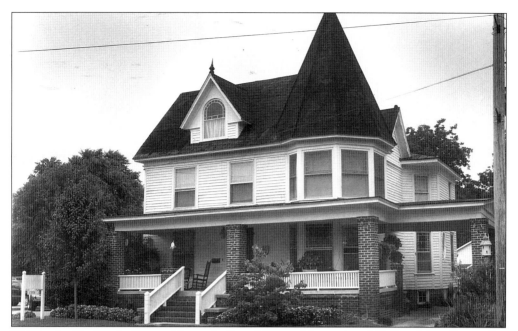

This is the Dr. Edwin Brown House, built *c.* 1885 and located at 140 East Main Street. Dr. Brown was one of a group of doctors who started the S.R. Fowle Memorial Hospital in 1902. Dr. Brown was appointed county health doctor in 1945. He and his sister Charlotte donated land for the Recreation Center on Charlotte Street. The Brown House is now owned by Roland and Martha Matthews Jr. (VC.)

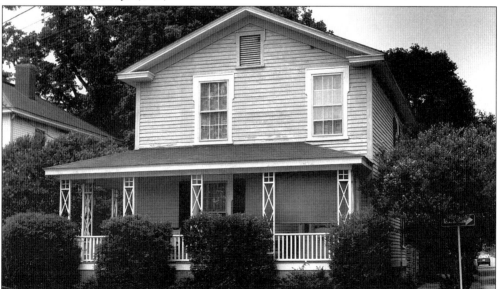

Living in a two-story plain gable end frame house at 164 East Main Street, Captain Alfred W. Styron made a panoramic photo of the Washington waterfront in 1875. He and Lawrence Clark owned the steam vessel *Edgecombe* until 1878. Styron ran a Marl Plant on Williamston Highway, where he had a kiln and dried and bagged marl—a mixture of clay and calcium carbonate—to sell to farmers as agricultural lime. The owners of the Styron House are now Marianna Franklin and Patricia Gertz. (VC.)

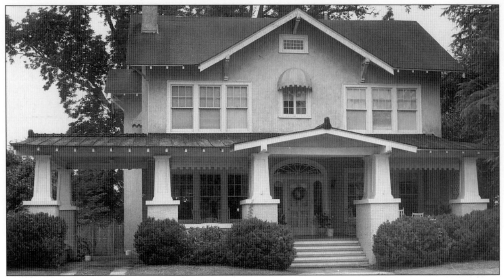

Located at 145 East Main Street, the C.M. Brown House was constructed *c.* 1918 as a two-story stuccoed home with Colonial Revival and bungalow details. A two-term mayor, Brown published the *North State Press* in 1879 and founded the Beaufort County Bank, which later became the First National Bank. Brown also developed the lower part of East Main, called Old Field in the 1890s, and he built the Brown building, with the Brown's Drug Store on the street floor and Brown's Opera House on the second floor. He had an old black horse called "Pet," and his carriage was painted tan. His daughter Charlotte, a pianist, married Frank Kugler, who owned Kulger Lumber Co. The Brown House is now owned by Robin and Zeno Edwards III. (VC.)

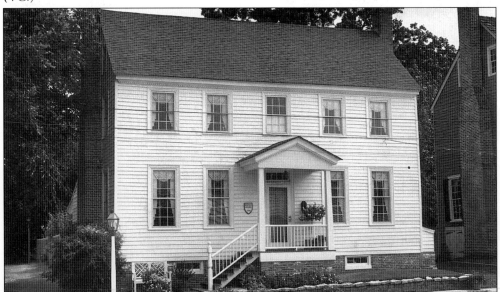

Located at 210 Water Street, the Marsh House was built *c.* 1795 by Daniel Gould Marsh and later owned by the Telfair family around 1855. Federal troops used this house and the Myers House, next door, as offices and quarters during the Civil War. Dallas and Adelia (Dee) Congelton restored this fine house in 1998. Notice the cannon ball lodged in the upper right facade, which was fired through the house during the Civil War. (VC.)

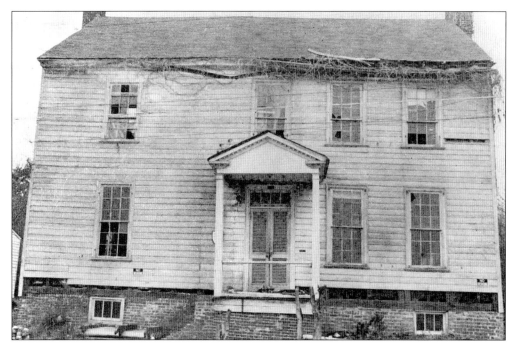

Located at 214 Water Street, the Myers House was one of three waterfront houses to survive the Civil War, the poverty of the Great Depression, and the razing of many historic sites to make way for progress. It was purchased by John Myers in 1826 and remodeled, and it remained in the family until 1976. In 1981, the home was restored by Herman Gaskins.

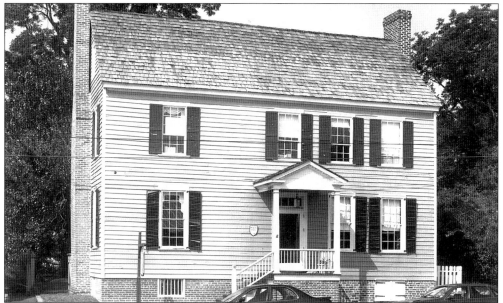

This is the restored Myers House, built *c.* 1760 and located at 214 Water Street. Myers and Son sold and leased steamboats to the Old Dominion Steamship Co. from 1872 to 1915. Their ships ran between Washington, Norfolk, and New York. They owned the *R.L. Myers*, the *Amidas*, the *Governor Morehead*, the *Cotton Plant*, the *Edgecombe*, the *Beaufort*, the *Annie Myers*, the *Lucy*, and the *Wilson*. (VC.)

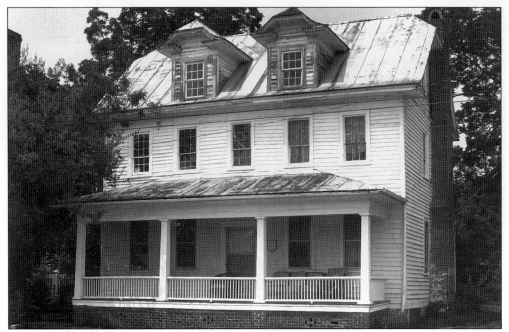

This is the Hyatt House, built *c.* 1785 at 222 Waters Street. The original house was a Federal-style structure built by an English sea captain. This house has been substantially altered with added ornamental dormers. Rumor has it that a ghost resides on the third floor. (VC.)

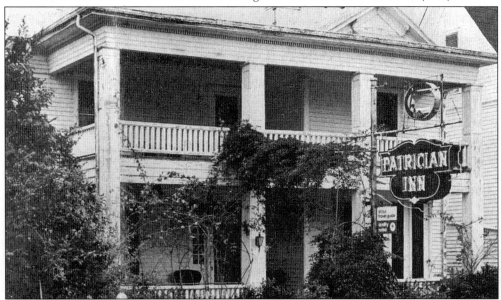

The Patrician Inn was built *c.* 1905 at 126 East Main Street. Originally called the Bragaw House, it was demolished in December 1971. Dave and Ellen Pickles turned it into a tearoom in 1928 and a 23-room inn in 1940. Mrs. Pickles furnished her rooms with a wonderful collection of worldly antiques. When the word got around, famous guests started to arrive—among them, actress Jennifer Jones (the wife of David Selznick), Gypsy Rose Lee, Susan Oliver, and James McArthur of *Hawaii Five-O* fame. Former Vice-President Alben W. Barkley spent his honeymoon here in the early 1950s. (WDN.)

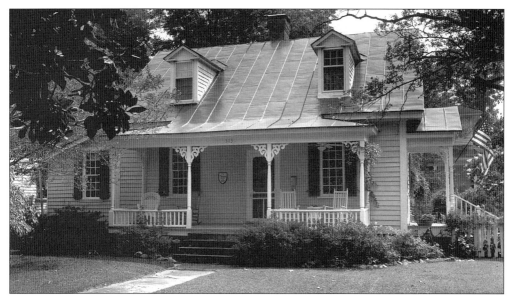

Local lore has it that the first surgery performed in Washington took place at the Thomas-Carter House, located at 303 East Main Street. This unusual one-and-half-story frame Cape Cod house has molded trim, dormer windows, 9-x-9 sash, a brick foundation, turned porch posts, and sawn trim. The original floor plan has been recreated using the home's original woodwork, four working fireplaces, three-room floors, and the windows. This charming house is owned by Carol and Charles Bowen. (VC.)

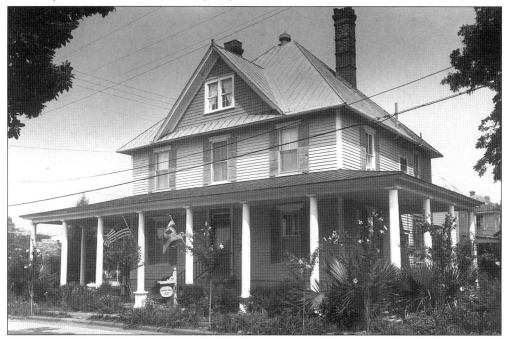

This is the Frank A. Moss House, built *c.* 1890 at 129 Van Norden Street. Moss was part owner of a lumber mill in Durhams Creek until 1918. This two-story, triple frame house has a columned porch on the front and left side. Now called the Acadian House Bed & Breakfast, it is owned by Leonard and Johanna Huber, innkeepers. (VC.)

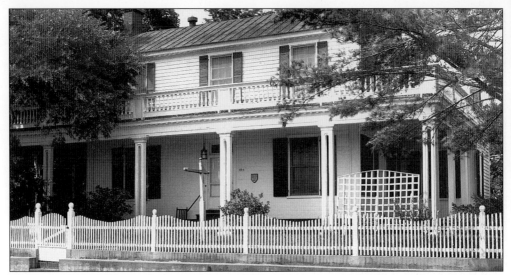

This is the Havens House, built c. 1820 at 404 West Main Street. The Havens family used their ancestral home, "Heartease," at Southold, Long Island, in New York, as a model. "Heartease" was patterned after a West Indies home which the Havens, who were shipping merchants, observed and admired while sailing their trade routes. The present owners are John and Elizabeth Hitt. (VC.)

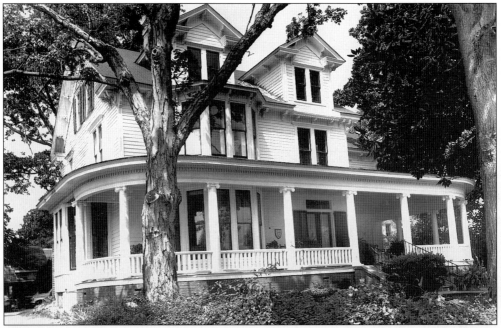

The Fowle House was built c. 1816 by W.H. Willard at 412 West Main Street and was used by Union troops as a Civil War hospital. Willard sold the property to Judge George Howard of Tarboro in 1877. Oscar Adams traded for a half interest and used his part of the house as a hotel. John Blackwell Fowle bought the house in 1888 and moved it back from the street, "from where it was just a short walk to the waterfront," said Elizabeth "Bee" Fowle Morton. The home remained in the family until 1999, when it was purchased by Jack and Wanda Morrow. (VC.)

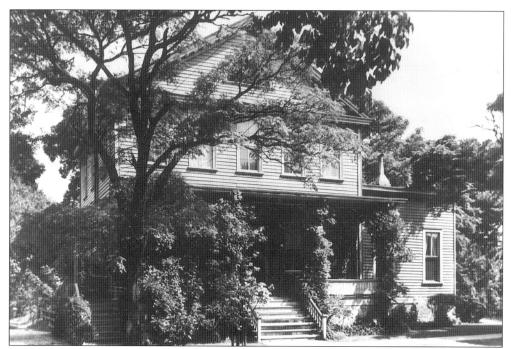

The Thomas Harvey Blount House, built *c.* 1860 at 321 North Market Street, was a very fine Federal-style, two-story frame house with a pedimented temple and early-nineteenth-century-style detail. This house was remodeled in 1937 and converted into offices in recent years. (VS.)

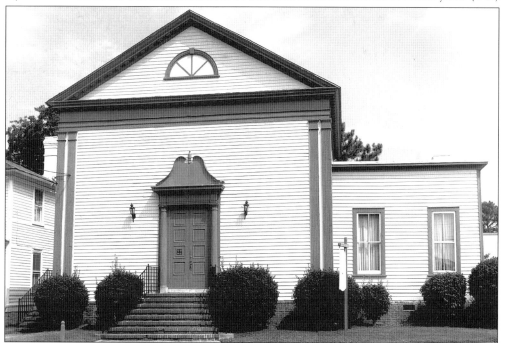

This is the Blount House, as shown above, after being remodeled a second time. It now has an attractive swan's neck pedimented entrance and serves as the offices of the Morris Insurance Agency. (VC.)

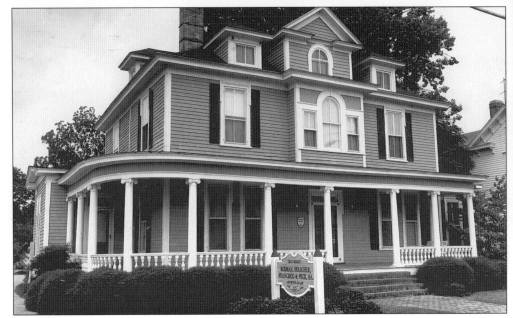

The Wilkens House, built *c.* 1884 at 320–322 North Market Street, is a two-and-a-half-story frame house with clipped gable dormers, a hipped roof, Palladian motif with wide Ionic type columns, and molded trim. Wilkens was a clerk of the courts. This house was remodeled around 1997, extended in the rear, and converted into offices for Rodman, Holscher, Francisco and Peck, PA. (VC.)

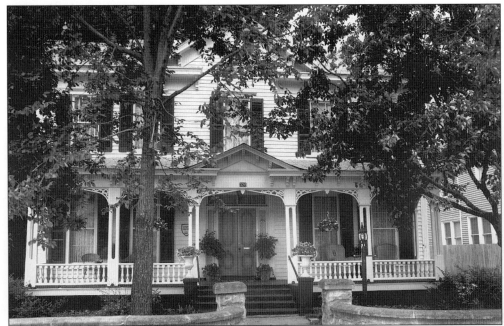

The E.W. Ayers House, constructed *c.* 1885 at 326 North Market Street, is a two-story, triple-A type frame house with bracketed detail and a porch with sawn and turned trim. Ayers had a dry goods store on Main Street in the early 1900s. The present owners are Roy and Virginia Bedard. (VC.)

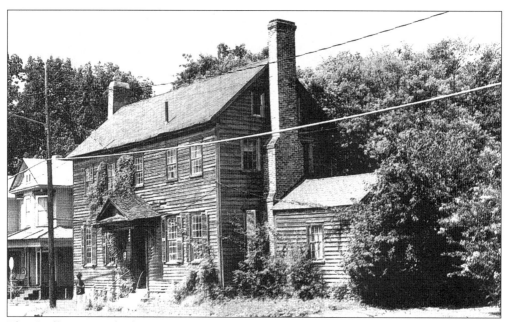

The Griffin House, built *c.* 1860 at 402 North Market Street, is one of the few antebellum Federal-style buildings to survive the Civil War. The outbuilding shares the chimney structure. (HPF.)

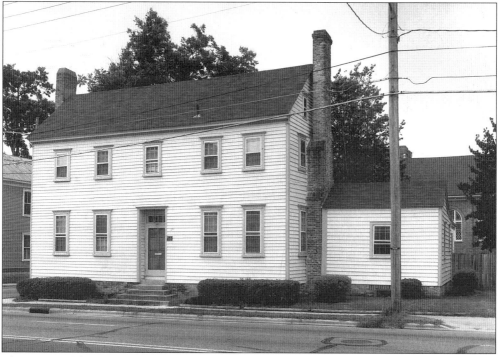

The owner of the Griffin House, seen here restored, was planning to tear it down in 1977 and sell the land. However, the Historic Preservation Fund of North Carolina bought an option and sold it to Hugh Todd for $18,000 in 1978. Mr. Todd made use of the Tax Reform Act of 1978, renovated the house, and created rental apartments. (VC.)

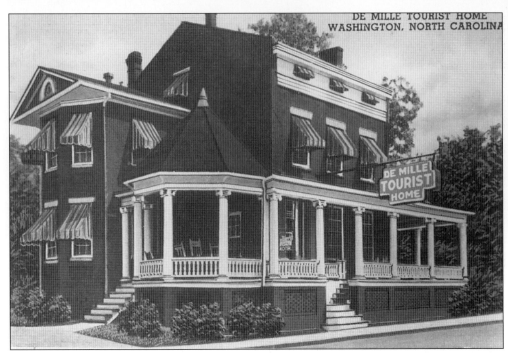

The DeMille House, built c. 1851 and demolished in 1953, was located on the corner of Bridge and Second Streets. Thomas DeMille, one of the founding fathers of St. Peter's Episcopal Church, built this elegant house as a wedding gift for William and Margaret DeMille. The first brick house built in Washington, it was a showplace for many years and was later purchased by J.K. Hoyt around 1900. (PC OS.)

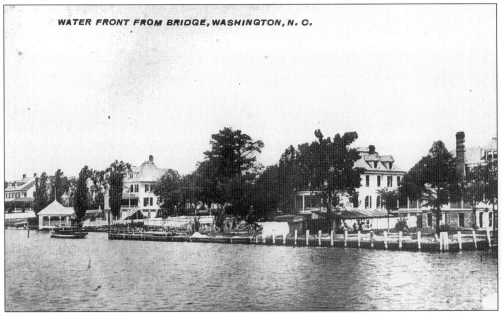

This waterfront scene was taken from the Pamlico River Bridge around 1912. The buildings are, from left to right, as follows: Riverside, the Dumay House, the Rodman House, and the Leach House. (PC SR.)

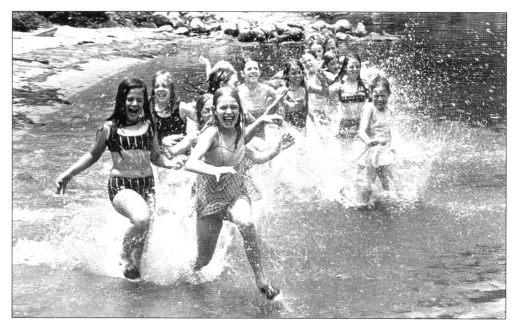

Here are the Camp Hardee Girl Scouts around 1950. These vibrant young ladies loved to swim and frolic along the river beach while at camp. (LT and BRL.)

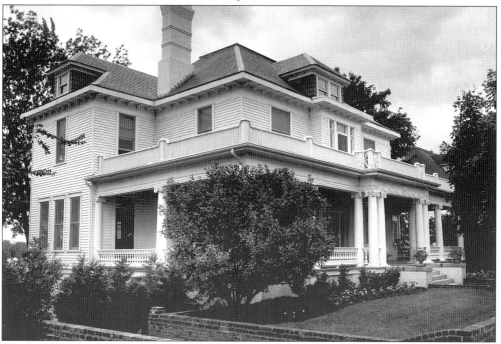

The Leach House, built *c.* 1879 at 501 West Main Street, is an impressive two-and-a-half-story Colonial Revival–style house with single and double paired Ionic type porch posts, bracketed cornice, and a hipped roof. Captain George T. Leach was president of Eureka Lumber Co., the largest lumber mill in Washington. In 1905, he organized the Washington and Vandermere Railroad, which ran to his mill. The present-day owners of the home are Jeffery and Anne Stuart Rumley. (VC.)

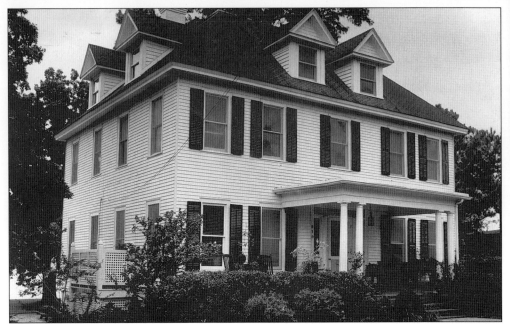

The Dr. John Rodman House, built c. 1904 at 519 West Main Street, is a two-and-a-half-story frame house with hipped roof, gable dormers, and an altered porch with Doric-type porch posts. Dr. Rodman was one of the founders of the S.R. Fowle Memorial Hospital in 1902. Present-day owners are Cheryl and Fredrick D. Austin III. (VC.)

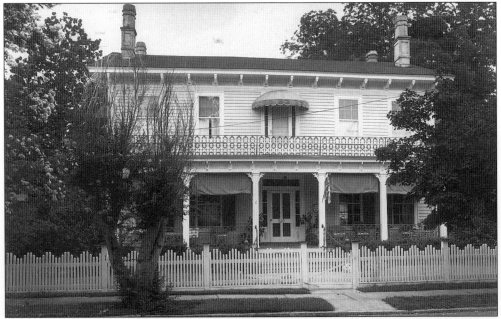

The Grist-Rodman House, built for John Grist c. 1848 at 520 West Main Street, is a frame house with Greek Revival and Italianate detail. It was purchased by Colonel William B. Rodman in 1867. A grandson, Judge W.B. Rodman III, who served as an associate justice of the Supreme Court from 1952 to 1962, lived here until his death. In 1999, the owner was Margaret Sloan Trainer. (VC.)

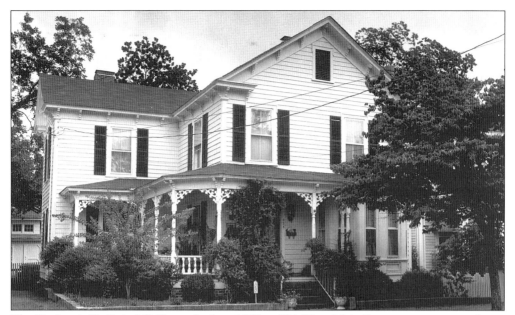

The Dr. Lewis H. Swindell House, built c. 1885 at 524 West Main Street, is a two-story frame house with Colonial Revival–style balusters. Coming to Washington in 1919, Dr. Swindell ran the Riverview Hospital until 1926 and then operated the Fowle Memorial Hospital from 1927 until the Beaufort County Hospital opened in 1958. The present-day owners are Marjorie and Richard L. Foree. (VC.)

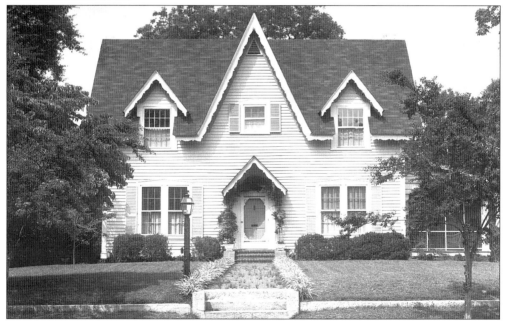

The Lindsay Warren House, built c. 1896 at 624 West Main Street, is a distinctive Gothic cottage with some Colonial Revival trim and notable sawn trim on the triple gable facade. Lindsay C. Warren was a U.S congressman and later a U.S. comptroller general. The house was built by his father for him. The present-day owners of the home are Lex and Linda Mann Jr. (VC.)

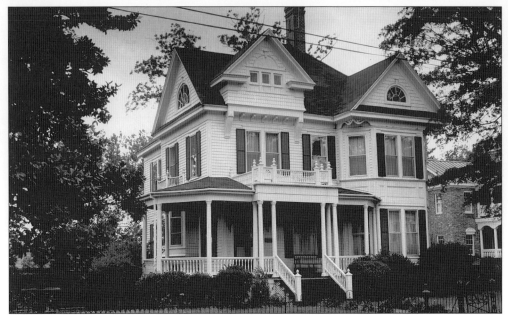

The A.M. DuMay House, built *c.* 1901 at 603 West Main Street, is a late-nineteenth-century Queen Ann–style frame house with shingle trim, gables on consoles, bay windows, a fine porch with vernacular porch posts, and a yard contained by a cast-iron fence and fountain. In 1897, DuMay and J.P. Jackson built a gas plant that replaced the one destroyed during the Civil War. DuMay was the cashier of the First National Bank. S.M. Mallison Jr. presently owns the home. (VC.)

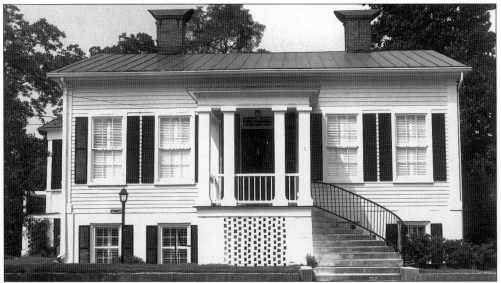

The Greenhill House, built *c.* 1825 at 612 West Main Street, was originally known as the Old Warren Place in 1850. An attractive one-story home built flush with the street and high off the ground, it was the home of Edward Jenner Warren, the grandfather of Lindsay C. Warren (page 102). Beneath the main floor is an old kitchen with a Dutch oven and great fireplace with hanging cranes, an English "housekeeper's" room, and a sewing room. The present-day owner is Philip W. Broome. (VC.)

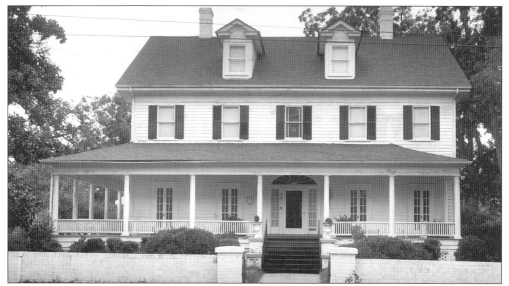

A Colonial Revival–style house, the Riverside-Winfield House, built c. 1886 at 627 West Main Street, was once a hotel and depot for Washington's first train—the *Jamesville and Washington*—laughingly called the "Jolt and Wiggle." One-half of the original house was moved to Jamesville and used as the depot for the northern end of the line. The present-day owner is Zelma M. Winfield. (VC.)

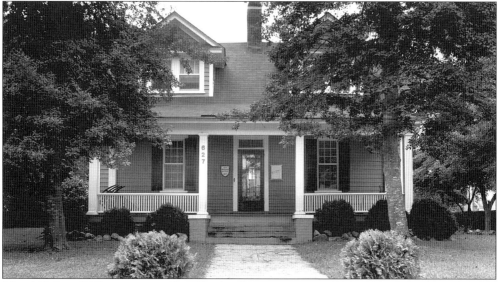

The Old Sam Williams Home Place, built c. 1857 at 627 West Second Street, is a pre–Civil War, one-and-a-half-story Colonial Revival–type house with fluted porch posts, 9-x-9 sash, pedimented dormers, and plain trim. This house was probably built by James H. Williams (1814–1872). His son Samuel Hodges Williams (1853–1908), a Washington merchant, owned it during his lifetime. Samuel Hodges Williams had five children—John Watkins Williams (1884–1953), Charles Morgan Williams (1886–1965), Samuel Hodges Williams Jr. (1889–1965), James Monroe Williams (1891–1972), and Margaret Elizabeth Williams. The home is now owned by Thomas and Heather Perry. (Text courtesy of Martha Williams Murry.) (VC.)

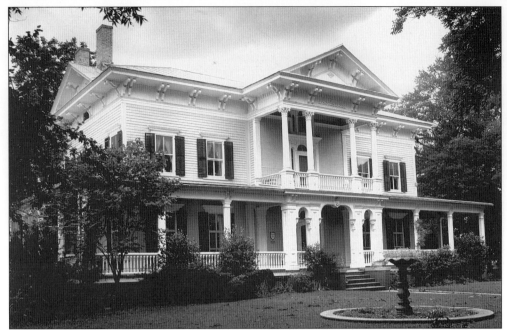

Elmwood, built by Colonel Joshua Tayloe c. 1820, is now located at 731 West Main Street. Elmwood began as a Federal-style home and in 1860 was enlarged to a two-story, double pile, Italianate residence. Later, many Colonial Revival embellishments were added including a wrap-around porch with a central two-story portico. Originally, Elmwood was located at the end of West Main Street, and the Gates of Elmwood faced downtown. Railroad tracks entered the edge of the property when the Grist family owned it. The house was moved to the south side of West Main Street in 1912 by its owner, buggy manufacturer George Hackney, to make way for the extension of West Main Street and the westward expansion of the City of Washington. The present-day owner is Mrs. Alice Stalling. (VC.)

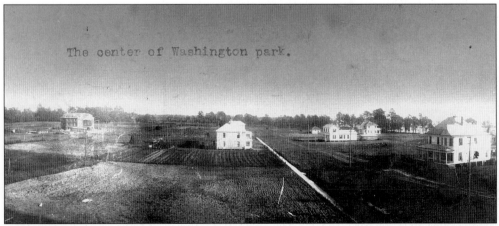

This is Washington Park with several homes under construction in 1913. From left to right are the Washington Collegiate Institute, the Warren House, the Shaw House, and the McMullan House (background). (WM.)

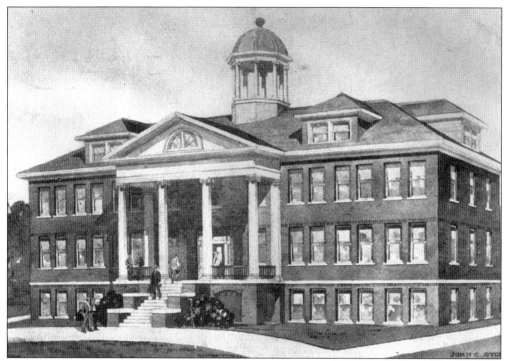

Washington Collegiate Institute (WCI), built c. 1913, was located on 20 acres of land in Washington Park, a subdivision of Washington. WCI was coed and was owned and managed by the Northern Methodist Church. Clay and Robena Carter were the first students enrolled. In 1919, WCI purchased an additional 50 acres and built a girls' dorm in 1921. The college closed during the 1930s depression. (WL.)

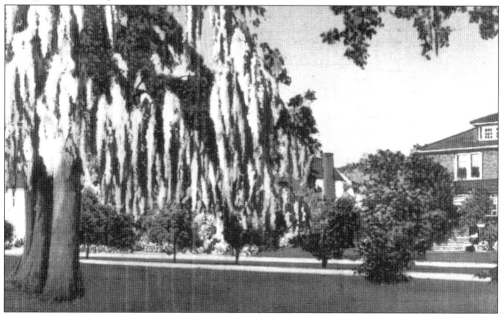

This live oak tree adorned with Spanish moss counterbalances the home at 304 Isabella Avenue in Washington Park around 1930. (PC OS.)

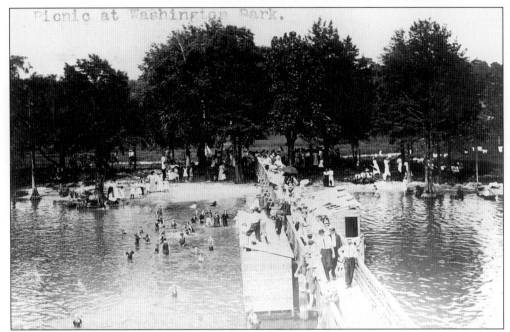

In 1923, Washington Park had 25 property owners. Owners and students of the Collegiate Institute bathed and frolicked at a community picnic held on the beach that borders Washington Park. (PC WM.)

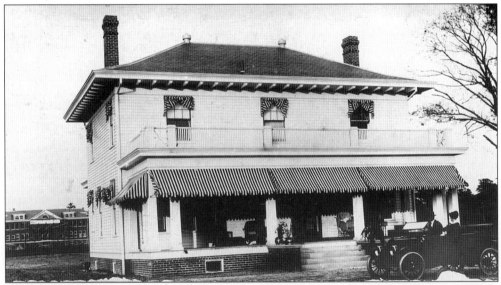

The H. McMullan House was built c. 1913 at 400 Riverside Drive in Washington Park. McMullan graduated from the University of North Carolina's Law School and moved to Washington in 1907 to join the law firm of Small & McLean. He married Pattie Baugham in 1911 and opened his own law office in 1913. In 1938, McMullan became attorney general of North Carolina and served in that position for 17 years until his death in 1955. Mildred McMullan Rumley inherited this house from her father, and she and her husband, Henry B. Rumley, sold their house, which was only a block away, and moved into the McMullan home in 1956. (HR.)

Six
TIMES FARMERS REMEMBER

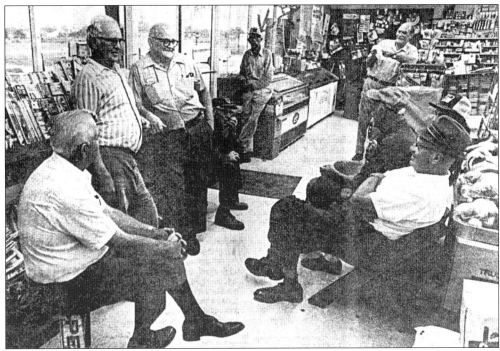

The "gang's all here" at Brooks grocery store in Bath in 1976. James Morgan, the owner, sold his grocery store in Bayview and bought the Brooks Store on Carteret Street next to Back Creek in 1978. Brooks says, "I only close two days a year, Thanksgiving and Christmas." The members of the "gang" may change from year to year, but even in the year 2000, they still gather to exchange fishing reports or compare crop harvest predictions. For these fellows, farming is their livelihood and the heart and soul of Beaufort County, and they are, from left to right, as follows: O.J. Gaylord, Vernon Godley Sr., Roy Brooks (next on stool), Jack Miller, Willie "Papa" Taylor, James Howard Brooks, Thorn Brooks, Jerry Paul, and Tom Pruitt. (LT; courtesy of VL.)

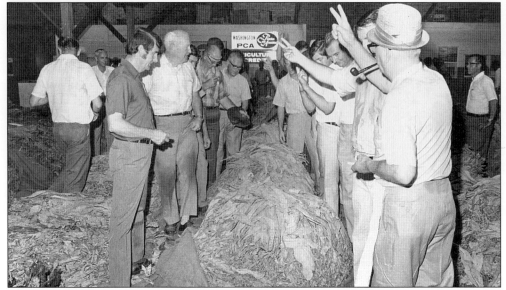

Pictured here is champion tobacco auctioneer Jimmy Hudson (first man, left row) working an auction in a Washington tobacco warehouse in 1970. Tobacco farming began in Beaufort County in 1896, when four county farmers—S.L. Grist, F.H. Von Eberstein, J.J. Laughinghouse, and T.R. Hodges—planted their first tobacco crops. They hauled their crops by mule-drawn carts to Danville, Virginia, to sell. Tobacco was then selling for 3¢ to 10¢ a pound. By 1900, enough farmers were growing the golden weed that Dr. Sam Tim Nicholson, a former Washington mayor, built a warehouse on the northeast corner of Seventh and Market Streets in Washington. (BRL.)

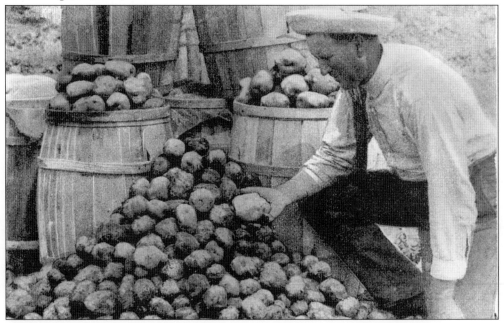

In 1910, early potatoes meant one could grow corn and other crops after the early spring potato harvest. The potatoes were then sorted and packed in barrels for shipping from the docks in Washington by water or rail transport. (PC OS.)

110

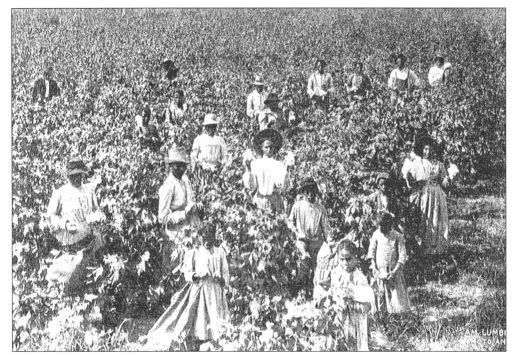

Across the bottom of this 1910 postcard was printed, "This cotton field produced one and one-half bales of ginned cotton per acre, after having matured a full crop of Irish potatoes in the spring." (PC OS.)

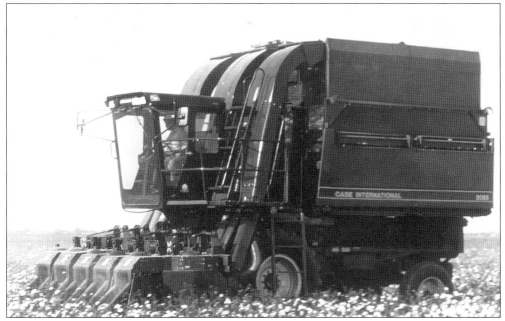

This Case International 2055 cotton picker is harvesting cotton in northern Beaufort County in the spring of 1993. "It takes three hours each day to prepare this machine for harvest," said Herb May of Mitchell Tractor & Equipment Co. "But, this machine can pick more in an hour than five workers can harvest by hand in a week." (MTE.)

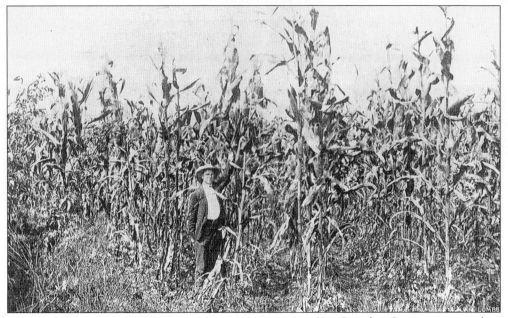

Yes, Beaufort County corn can be as high as an elephant's eye. This 1910 "second crop corn" scene attested to the quality of Eastern North Carolina farm soil at the beginning of the twentieth century. (PC OS.)

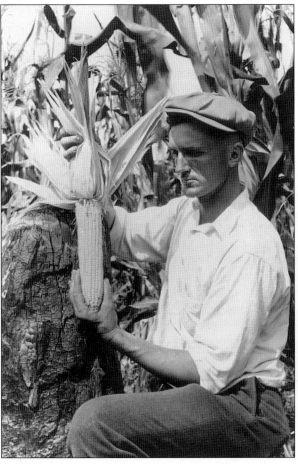

This proud, unidentified farmer shows off the quality of his corn crop in 1920. (WM.)

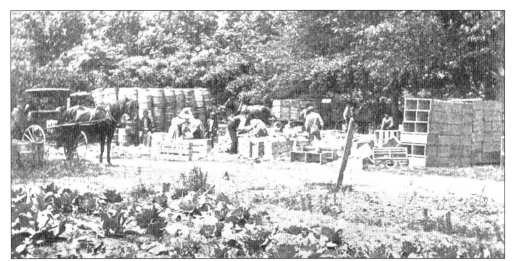

Hand-picked cabbage is being packed for shipment to the Northern market. This picture indicates that they used both barrels and crates for packing. Cabbage was grown extensively in Beaufort County in 1915. (WL.)

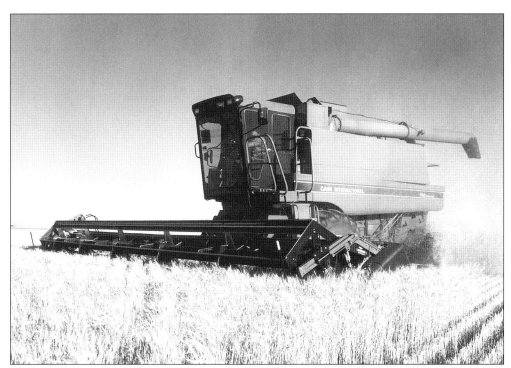

This Case International 1688 combine is harvesting wheat in Beaufort County in the spring of 1994. The wide leader in front cut the wheat stalk and sent it into the machine that separated the kernel from the chaff. "This machine could harvest 100 acres per day, compared to the old hand sickle method that might take a month," said Herb May. (MTE.)

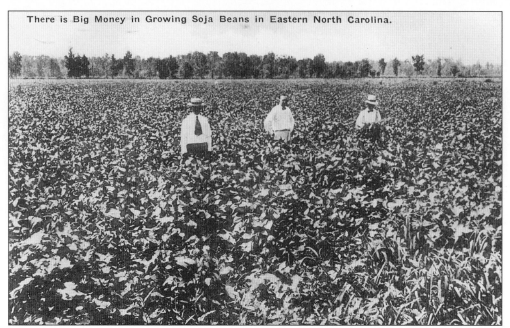

There is "Big Money" in growing Soya beans in Eastern North Carolina claimed this 1912 postcard. Notice the unusual spelling for "Soya," or for "Soybeans." (PC OS.)

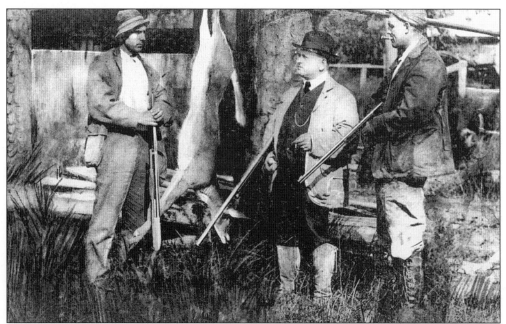

Hunting seems to be every farmers' favorite off-season pastime, and so it was with President Grover Cleveland, who came to Washington on the USCG buoy tender *Violet* in 1897. Charles Warren wanted to honor Cleveland's arrival, but the president wanted none of it, saying "I came to Washington to go hunting and fishing." The next day, he and Warren went hunting in Hyde County. This photograph is believed to show President Grover Cleveland (center) with Charles Warren and an unknown companion. (PC OS.)

Seven

TIMES WORTH
REMEMBERING

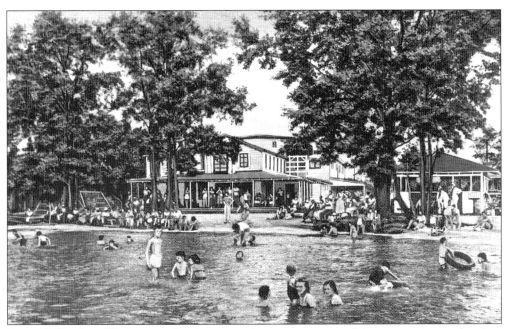

From 1947, when Washington families wanted to go swimming, fishing, camping, or boating, they did not have far to travel. Whichard's Beach Campground & Marina in Chocowinity supplied it all. This fine campground has been damaged several times by storms, including 1999, but the owners always rebuilt because they love the area. (PC OS.)

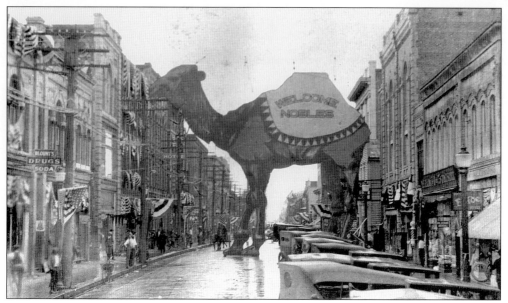

For the 1926 Shriner's parade, Jessie Giles and Ike Hughes built and painted a three-story-high camel in Gravely's Tobacco Warehouse to welcome the Nobels. The camel straddled Main Street and was suspended by guy wires stretched across the street between the Harris Hardware building and the New Theater on West Main Street. (PC LL.)

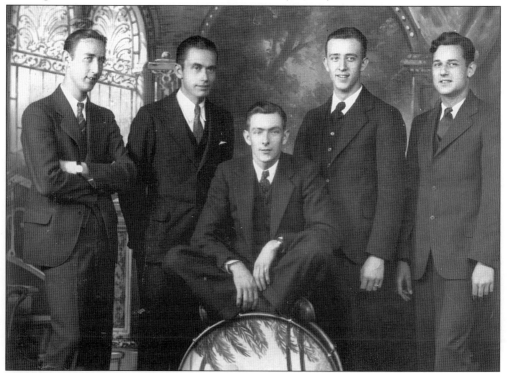

Washington has never lacked for musical entertainment. Here are the Five Troubadores in 1931; they are, from left to right, as follows: Ed Stevenson (bass), Hugh Phillips (piano), Henry B. Rumley (drums), Vernon Stevenson (trumpet), and Raymond Walters (sax). (PC HR.)

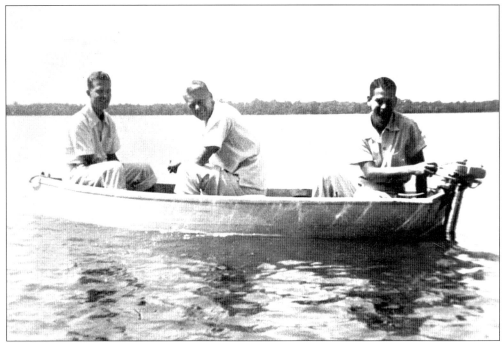

Gerald Ford (center) came to Washington in the summer of 1937, when he was a student at the University of North Carolina's Law School. Ford had made friends with Harry McMullan Jr. (right) and Julian Warren (left), who were also students. The three "buddies" went fishing on the Pamlico River behind the McMullan home on Riverside Drive in Washington Park. (HR.)

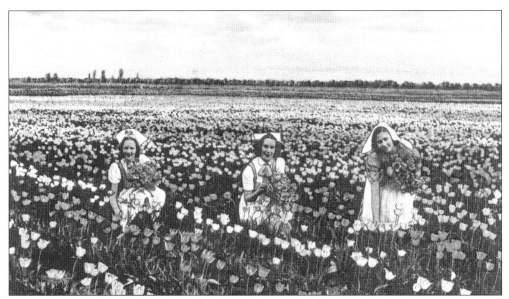

Each spring from 1937 to 1941, Washington held a weekend Tulip Festival. This event was inspired by Mrs. Olive Rumley, an editor at the *Washington Daily News*. Mrs. Rumley said, "Let's hold a weekend folk festival as a salute to the Dutch families of Terra Ceia who raise hundreds of acres of tulips and daffodils." World War II interrupted this fun event, and it was never resumed. (PC OS.)

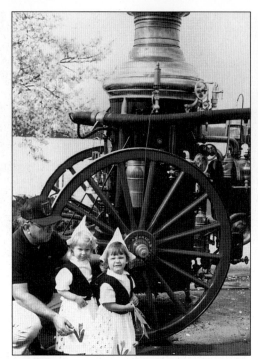 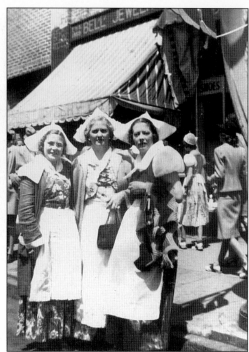

Left: The fire department's old 1898 horse-drawn steamer was always a part of the Tulip Festival Parade. Here is fireman Huge Sterling and his "cute as a button" daughters, Cindy and Beth, enjoying the event. (WFD.) *Right:* The Tulip Festival featured folk singing by the Dutch of Terra Ceia (dressed in their native costumes), band concerts, boat races, a baby and a pet parade, and a grand parade with pretty girls from throughout Beaufort County. The girls displayed their lovely costumes as they traveled on elaborately decorated floats down Main Street. (VS.)

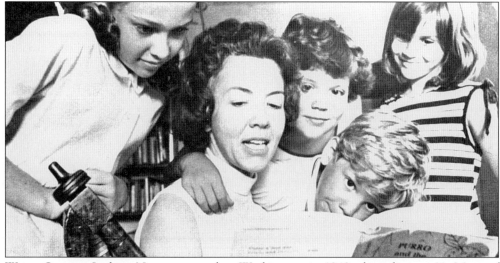

Writer Suzanne Latham Newton moved to Washington in 1948 when she was 11. Many of Suzanne's childhood memories appear in her writing. "A good bit of what I've written has had the river and the peacefulness of the river in it," she said. Suzanne is best known for *What Are You Up To, William Thomas?* (1977). (OP.)

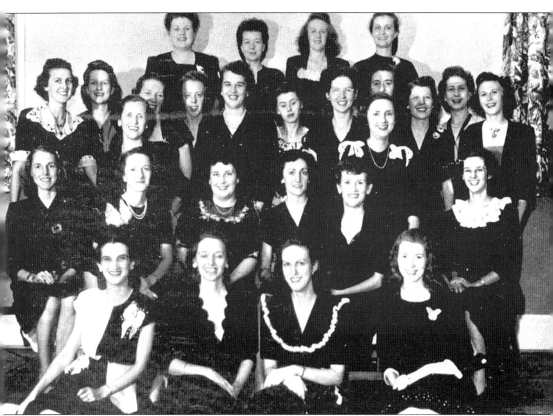

In 1941, during World War II, some of the lovely women of Washington formed a social club called the "Spinsters." The group first met in Rodman and Rodman's law offices, on the second floor of the Mecca Billiards Hall at 129 North Market Street. They are, from left to right, as follows: (front row) Joyce Swain Ray, Ella Waters Pfau, Jane Blount, and Anita Koonce Tyndall; (second row) Lola Mae Phillips Metts, Elizabeth Berry Hoffler, Lala Bragaw, Tay Fowle Carter, Roberta Stephenson Snell, and Elizabeth Fowle Morton; (third row) Rebecca Vaughan Ellsworth, Eva Blount Kornegay, Carlotta Waters, Margaret Hodges Himmelwright, Rena Harding Davenport, Anice Harding Tripp, Mary Diamond Gray, Mary Elizabeth Robbins Judd, Frances Gardner Snyder, Doris Weston Gibbs, Betsy Bowers Litchfield, Mary Helen Rodman Hill, and Emily Bryan Squires Tunstall; (fourth row) Jean Taylor Heath, Mary Ross Vester, Julia Latham Mitchell, and Verna Tyson Attmore. (TC.)

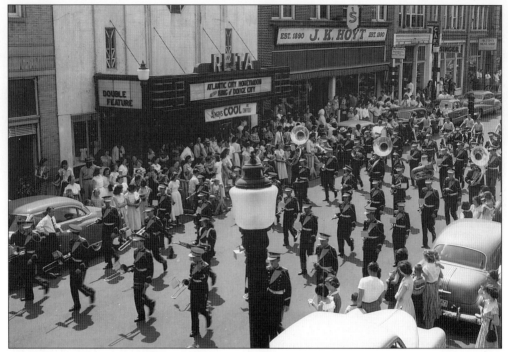

Regardless of the season, Washingtonians have always enjoyed a good parade. Here is our popular Washington High School Marching Band strutting down Main Street past the Reita Theatre (formerly the Strand) during the 1951 Summer Festival. (VS.)

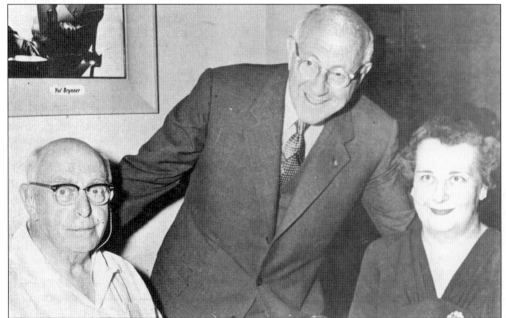

Cecil B. DeMille (middle) chats with Lalla Bragaw and her father, John, in Hollywood in August 1957. DeMille was not born in Washington but was raised here. DeMille's inspiration for his *King of Kings* movie came from sitting opposite a portrait of the *Last Supper*, which hung over the dining room mantel in his home on Bridge Street. (BRL.)

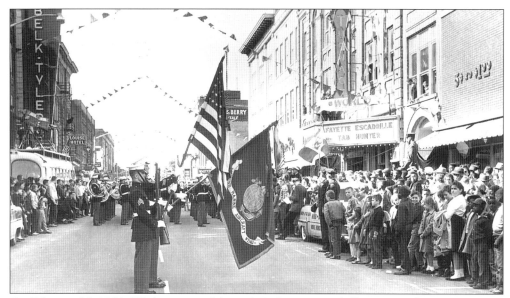

On February 28, 1958, Washington celebrated "Lafayette Escadrille Day," to honor Sgt. James Baugham, the youngest American member of the French Escadrille air squadron. Baugham was killed in action in 1918. The Second Marine Aircraft Wing Band led a parade that was followed by an air show at Warren Airport. The world premiere movie, starring Tab Hunter as Jim Baugham, was shown at the Turnage Theatre at 8 p.m. Proceeds went to a "Jim Baugham Lafayette Escadrille" memorial youth center fund. (TS.)

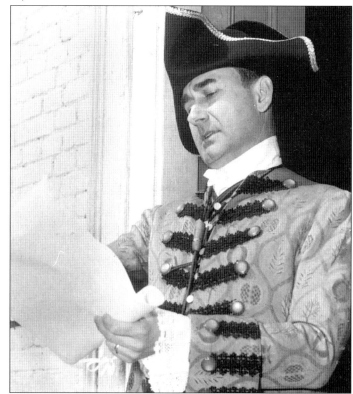

Mayor Thomas Stewart played the "town crier" and proclaimed the week of March 24, 1960, to be Tercentenary Week, in commemoration of the 300th birthday of the granting of the charter of the land that became the colonies. Thomas Stewart was mayor for 14 years—from 1957 to 1971. (TS.)

121

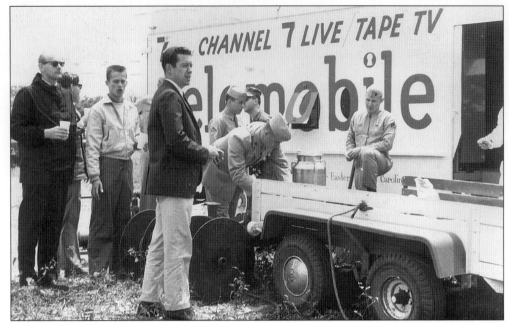

In 1965, Channel-7 TV was both an ABC and an NBC affiliate station. TV-7 was owned by W.R. Roberson Jr., who also owned WRRF Radio and several Dr. Pepper franchises. Pictured here is Channel-7's first Live Tape TV Telemobile truck on location at the Marine Corps Station in Jacksonville, North Carolina. From left to right are Robert McCoy; Carl Rochell, engineer (now with CNN); Bowman Lewis, production manager (now director of the Washington Beaufort County Chamber of Commerce); and Peeve Nobles. (BL.)

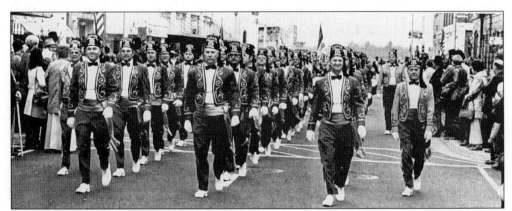

The Sudan Temple Shrine Marching Band swings down Main Street on November 20, 1976. This parade was the highlight of the Togo Wynne Fall Ceremonial held in Beaufort County. Some 200 candidates were initiated in Sudan Temple ceremonies at the Washington High School. The Shriners contribute generously every year to the Crippled Children's Fund. (BRL.)

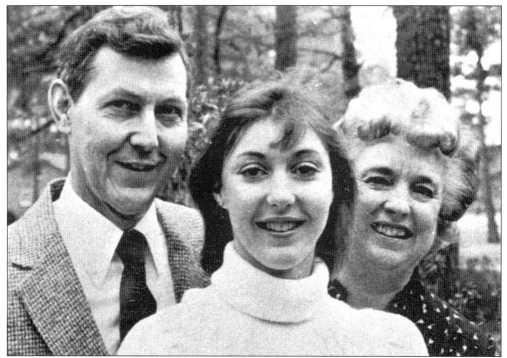

Maureen Stevens (seen with her parents) graduated from Washington High School in 1975. Maureen was chosen Miss Beaufort County in 1979. In 1983, she was a member of a temporary Los Angeles company of Rocketts who presented *The Christmas Spectacular* before disbanding in December. "It was so exciting to be in the first company of Rocketts, besides the original New York group," said Maureen. (CG.)

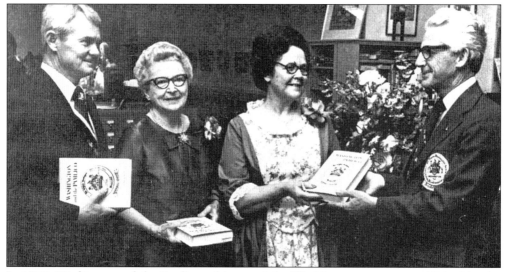

In 1976, *Washington and the Pamlico*, a history of the Washington area, was published by the Washington-Beaufort County Bicentennial Commission. Pictured are co-editors Ursula Loy (second from right), Pauline Worthy, and John Morgan (History Committee chairman) accepting their official copies from Bicentennial Commission chairman Roland Modlin. More than 300 residents attended the March 15th ceremony at the Brown Library. (WDN.)

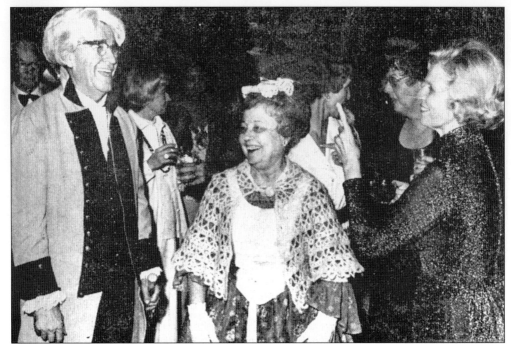

The City of Washington observed its 200th anniversary on February 23, 1976. More than 250 residents gathered at Brentwood Lodge for an evening of entertainment. Chairman Stancil Lilley (on the left) attracted considerable attention as he and Mrs. A.N. Sawyer sported colonial garb. They are shown here chatting with Mrs. Harold Lane. (TS.)

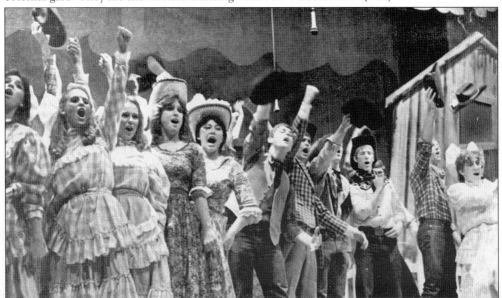

Washingtonians always enjoy a rootin' tootin' musical. "Oklahoma! Yeow!" rang out the final chorus to a standing ovation at the Washington High School performance on March 23, 24, 25, and 26, 1983. Pam Rogers played Aunt Eller, Thomas Davenport was Curley, and Shannon Oughton was Laurey. Some 60 students sang and danced their hearts out and found togetherness during this rousing show. (OP.)

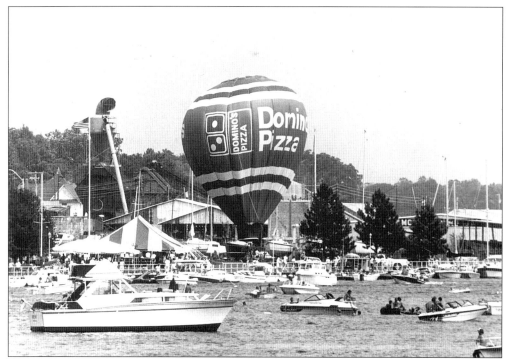

The Pamlico River was a busy place in Washington for the 1988 Summer Festival. Seen from the river view, from left to right, are the Hyatt House (white), Moss Planing Mill (the dark building with the tall smoke stack), Pamlico Marine, and a portion of Moss Planing. (BRL.)

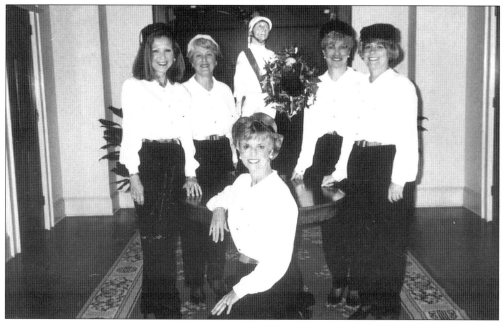

The Pamlico Sounds, in April 1988, sang for a Hospital Foundation volunteer luncheon at the Jockey Club in Greenville. From left to right are Cindy Horner, Linda Seale, Jan Hindsley, Tish Moore, and Teresa Mays (center). (TH.)

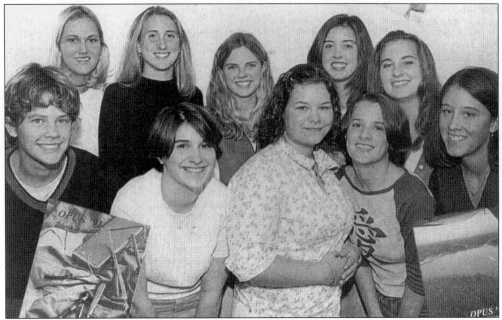

The editorial staff at Washington High School has published *Opus* magazine annually since 1981. Here is the 1999 *Opus* staff, directed by Susan Wellborn (not shown); they are, from left to right, as follows: (front row) Heather Moore, Kathleen Roberson, Michelle Hooper, Heather Woolard, and Jennifer Price; (back row) Cameron Buckman, Natalie Cherry, Emily Atkins, Landas Woolard, and Casey Edwards. (RW WDN.)

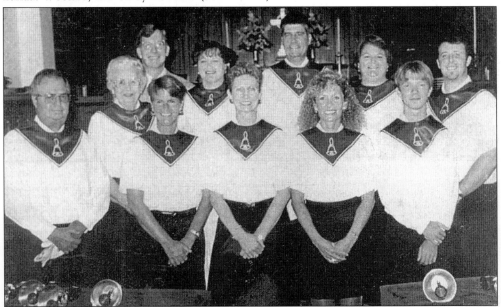

On Sunday, August 22, 1999, the Chancel Bells of the First United Methodist Church presented their summer concert "Showstoppers" at the Washington Civic Center. From left to right are the following: (front row) Allen Love, Marsha Bowes, Laveita Brinson, Carolyn Wetmore, and Frankie Myers; (second row) Lois Sawyer, Tom Secor, Kaye Buckman, Alan Corell, Penny Cowan, and Al Secor. (RW WDN.)

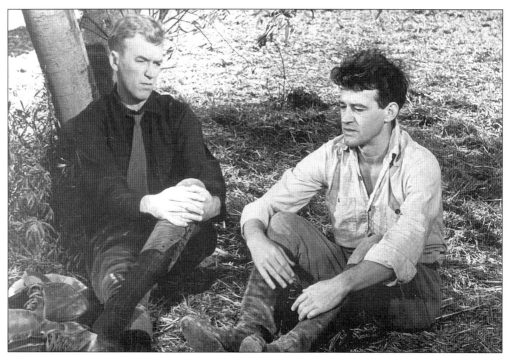

Hollywood actor Murray Hamilton was born in Washington in 1923, the son of George "Fate" and Minnie Corelia Honeycut Hamilton. At age 18, he hopped a bus to Hollywood, where he eventually caught on as an actor. He played opposite Jimmy Stewart in *Spirit of Saint Louis*, Henry Fonda in *Mister Roberts*, Tab Hunter in *The Girl He Left Behind*, and Rock Hudson in *Seconds*, and he played the lead in *The FBI Story*, as Special Agent Sam Crandall. (Photo by Mac Julian; courtesy "Rusty" Walker.)

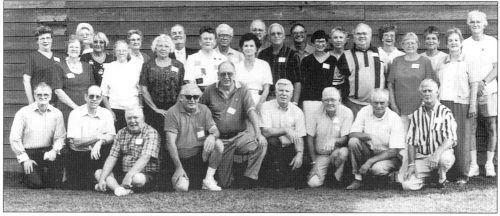

The 1999 reunion of the Bath High School Class of 1954 includes the following, from left to right: (first row) Gene Foreman, Donald Wallace, C.E. Tetterton, Carl Tetterton, Jimmy Mason, Thomas Foskey, Marlow Paul, Jasper Woolard, and Sammy Woolard; (second row) Zelma Singleton, Carol Keech, Gertrude Wallace, Frances Rose, Geraldine Respass, Teeny Mason, Joyce Huguelet, Howard Cutler, Eunice Woolard, and Lois Perry; (third row) Barbara Sanderson, Betty Hardee, Mary Faye Wallace, Vernetta Lange, Jasper Swain, Adrian McGown, Bobby Swindell, Kent Gurganus, Sybil Leary, Frances Latham, Mary Frances Woolard, and George Nelson. (TH, courtesy VL.)

ACKNOWLEDGMENTS

Historic preservation has been of interest to me for many years, probably because I handled so many architectural assignments during my professional photography career from 1949 to 1985. I decided to try my hand at producing an up-to-date pictorial history of Washington. My plan became a reality when Linda Oden, of Oden's Store at Hunter's Ridge, agreed to let me copy her excellent postcard collection. Then Louis G, May, Bowman Lewis, Henry B. Rumley, William Mayo, Thomas Stewart, Warren Lane, Vann's Studio, Louise Lane, and Ashley Futrell also supplied me with many additional interesting images. I did some historic research, and after several months of writing and photography, my diligent wife, Vera, tendered her editorial and editing acumen, and H. Blount Rumley Jr., Fred Mallison, Penelope Rodman, Bee Morton, Elizabeth Sterling, and Hugh Sterling did the proofreading. Vance Harper Jones contributed additional information for this second edition. So here is my pictorial heritage version of twentieth-century Washington. I hope you enjoy it.

Photo/Image Credits
(Symbol PC = Postcard from)

AF	Ashley Futrell	OP	*Opus* magazine
AR	Abe Ricter	OS	Oden's Store
BHM	BHM Regional Library	RW	Russell Walker
BK	W.H. Baker	SR	Stuart Rumley
BL	Bowman Lewis	ST	Scotty Taylor, Fire Dept.
BRL	Brown Library	TC	Mrs. Tim Carter
CC	Clay Carter	TH	Tim Hanifer, Creative Video
CCX	Cathy Cox	TS	Thomas Stewart
CG	Chip Goebert	VC	Louis Van Camp
DHY	Drucilla Haley York	VL	Vernetta Lange
DM	Mrs. Duncan Moore	VS	Vann's Studio
ES	Elizabeth Sterling	WDN	*Washington Daily News*
HR	Henry B. Rumley	WFD	Washington Fire Department
HPF	Historic Preservation Fund of NC	WL	Warren Lane
IN	Inglis 1915	WM	William Mayo
KS	Karen Stocks	WS	William Sellers
LL	Louise Lane	WT	Whiting Toler
LM	Louis G. May	WY	Washington Yacht Club
LT	Leslie Todd	ZH	Zena Hodges
MTE	Mitchell Tracter Co.		

Source books: *Washington on the Pamlico*; *The Old North State, Historical Highlights of Washington and Beaufort County*; *Pen and Picture Sketches of 1915, Washington North Carolina*; *The National Register of Historic Places Inventory-Washington, NC*; *Beaufort County Magazine*; *Opus* magazine; *Early History of Washington Park*; *Washington & Beaufort County Nineteen Hundred Thirteen*; and *Growing Up on the Old Norfolk Southern*. Storefronts and home locations were accessed from the *National Register of Historic Places—Washington, North Carolina*. This information was supplied by the City of Washington Planning and Development Department. The author takes no responsibility for the accuracy of source material.